First Course Review

Second Edition

Bryan Coombs

Pitman

PITMAN PUBLISHING LIMITED
128 Long Acre, London WC2E 9AN

Associated Companies
Pitman Publishing Pty Ltd, Melbourne
Pitman Publishing New Zealand Ltd, Wellington

© Pitman Publishing Limited 1982

First edition 1976
Second edition 1982
Reprinted 1982, 1983 (twice), 1984

Text set in 10/12 pt Linotron 202 Bembo.
Printed in Great Britain at The Pitman Press, Bath

ISBN 0 273 01801 9

PREFACE

This book aims to re-present the theory in a precise but thorough manner using new and copious examples of each principle; to review short forms and phrases; and to give continuous practice passages for consolidation of the theory and extension of vocabulary.

Each unit contains theory revision, a theory drill, short forms and practice material in the form of correspondence and/or a short continuous passage.

Study Plan

A revision and consolidation of theory will be achieved by working through this book. Although it is not essential to cover each unit in the order presented it is important to revise in a systematic manner. However, if there is a marked weakness in certain areas of theory which need urgent attention these may be revised first.

All new examples of the theory should be read, understood and practised until they become totally familiar. The short forms, intersections and phrases should already have been mastered from *First Course* (second edition). Any of these outlines not already learned to the point of instantaneous recall should be given special attention.

The drills and other continuous material should be read through several times. Any outline causing hesitancy should be checked with the key which follows each shorthand exercise, and then thoroughly drilled. A fair copy of each passage should be made, writing for both accuracy and speed. Finally, each piece of material should be written from dictation several times, with any remedial work taking place between each dictation. A word count is given in brackets at the end of each exercise.

The aim of all reading and writing exercises is to recognize, read and write each outline accurately and quickly, and to improve the reading and writing skill at each repetition. What is read is seen, and when it is read again and again the shorthand outline that was seen is associated with the word. When that same word is heard later the shape of the outline is remembered and written instantly. After the first, and possibly slow, reading and writing of any outline there must be a concentration on speed as well as accuracy. Accurate outlines build penmanship confidence and speed in writing follows. Accurate notes are essential for rapid and precise transcription.

No addresses are included in the correspondence material. Students should compose addresses to make their transcriptions realistic.

CONTENTS

CHAPTER 1

Position Writing
Diphones
The omission of vowels
Figures, Currency, Dates
Times, Temperatures

POSITION WRITING

First Position

The first upstroke or downstroke of an outline is written *above* the line:

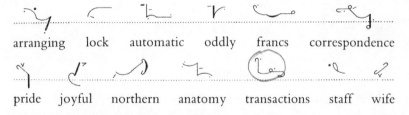

arranging   lock   automatic   oddly   francs   correspondence

pride   joyful   northern   anatomy   transactions   staff   wife

When the outline consists entirely of horizontal strokes it is written *above* the line:

clause   annoy   knocker   crag   stamina   maximum   graft   classical

Second Position

The first upstroke or downstroke of an outline is written *to* or *from* the line:

famous   celebrate   receipt   breath   fresh   furniture   broke

1

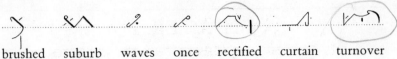

brushed　suburb　waves　once　rectified　curtain　turnover

When the outline consists entirely of horizontal strokes it is written *on* the line:

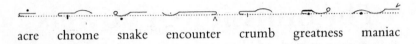

acre　chrome　snake　encounter　crumb　greatness　maniac

Third Position

The first upstroke or downstroke of an outline is written *through* the line:

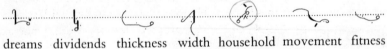

dreams　dividends　thickness　width　household　movement　fitness

reality　liaison　crystallize　disobedient　international　complete

When the outline consists entirely of horizontal strokes it is written *on* the line:

screaming　gleaming　minimum　scrutinize　goodness　mini　newcomer

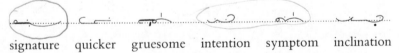

signature　quicker　gruesome　intention　symptom　inclination

DIPHONES

This double vowel sign ..._ᵥ_.. indicating one vowel sound following another, is placed in the position of the first of these two vowel sounds:

theatre　media　curious　ideology　junior　creation　really　million

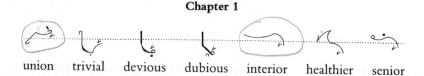

union	trivial	devious	dubious	interior	healthier	senior

THE OMISSION OF VOWELS

In this book vowels are shown in the theory drills but only the essential vowels in the practice material. Outlines do not always need to be fully vocalized, and the writer must decide which essential vowels should be written. Accurate position writing allows the writer to omit many vowels. It is essential to place the first upstroke or downstroke (or the first horizontal, in outlines consisting only of horizontal strokes) in the correct position.

At the beginning or at the end of an outline, the presence or absence of a vowel is sometimes indicated by the use or non-use of a full stroke consonant, or final hook, or loop or circle. By writing a full stroke in some outlines there is no need to place a vowel:

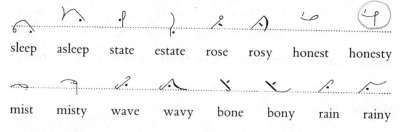

sleep	asleep	state	estate	rose	rosy	honest	honesty

mist	misty	wave	wavy	bone	bony	rain	rainy

The correct use of upward **R** and downward **R** indicates the presence or absence of an initial or a final vowel:

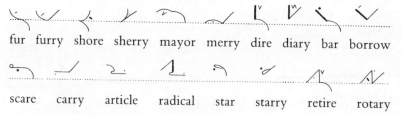

fur	furry	shore	sherry	mayor	merry	dire	diary	bar	borrow

scare	carry	article	radical	star	starry	retire	rotary

Single stroke outlines which have an initial and a final vowel usually need to have the final vowel indicated, and in some cases both vowels are necessary:

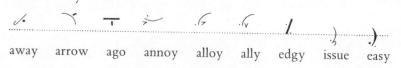

away	arrow	ago	annoy	alloy	ally	edgy	issue	easy

Chapter 1

An outline consisting only of a half-length stroke should be vocalized:

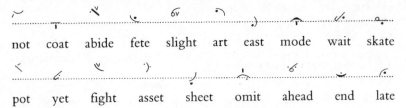

| not | coat | abide | fete | slight | art | east | mode | wait | skate |

| pot | yet | fight | asset | sheet | omit | ahead | end | late |

The diphthongs **I, OI, OW, U,** and triphones should be inserted to aid transcription:

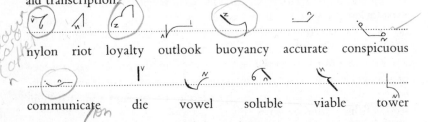

| nylon | riot | loyalty | outlook | buoyancy | accurate | conspicuous |

| communicate | die | vowel | soluble | viable | tower |

When two outlines have the same pattern of consonants it is important to vocalize one of them, usually the less frequently occurring outline:

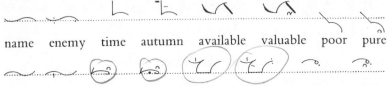

| name | enemy | time | autumn | available | valuable | poor | pure |

| many | money | human | humane | unlikely | unluckily | amazing | amusing |

An unusual outline should be fully vocalized the first time it is written. If the word is repeated during the dictation it will not be necessary to vocalize the outline in full again.

FIGURES

In straightforward continuous matter and for round numbers write shorthand outlines for the following numerals:

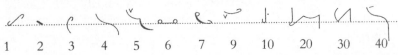

| 1 | 2 | 3 | 4 | 5 | 6 | 7 | 9 | 10 | 20 | 30 | 40 |

Above 10 write Arabic numerals. 0 and 8 are always written as Arabic numerals.

Single numerals followed by a specific unit of measurement, or currency, are written as numerals:

3 pints 4 litres 7 tons/tonnes 5 ounces 8 grammes 2 kilogrammes

Stroke **P** can be used for *per cent* when combined with a numeral:

8 per cent   15 per cent   2½ per cent

CURRENCY

Write the shorthand outline ⤳ for *pounds*:

£5   £8.20   £21.05   £6,000   £500,000   £3,000,000

Add **circle S** to the short form for *dollar*   to represent *dollars*:

$5,000 $100 $8,000,000

For all other currencies write the shorthand outlines:

2,000 lire   900 francs   35 marks   600 pesetas   7 guilders

DATES

6 January   8th May   22nd April 1982   21st October 1984

23rd November   14th February   1st August

TIMES

16.30 hours   4 p.m.   09.00 hours   8 a.m.   5 o'clock   2 o'clock

Chapter 1

TEMPERATURES

It is not advisable to write the usual longhand abbreviations for centigrade and Fahrenheit when writing shorthand from dictation. Temperatures are best expressed as follows:

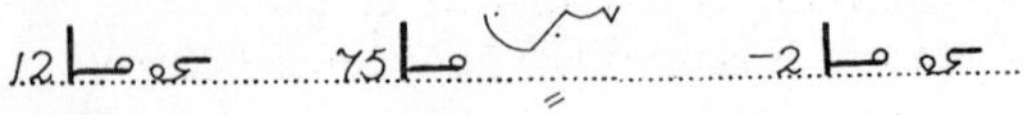

12°C   75°F   −2°C

THEORY DRILL

1 (22)

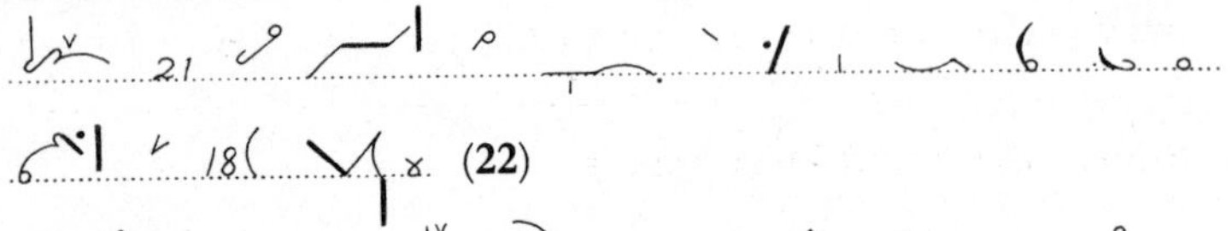

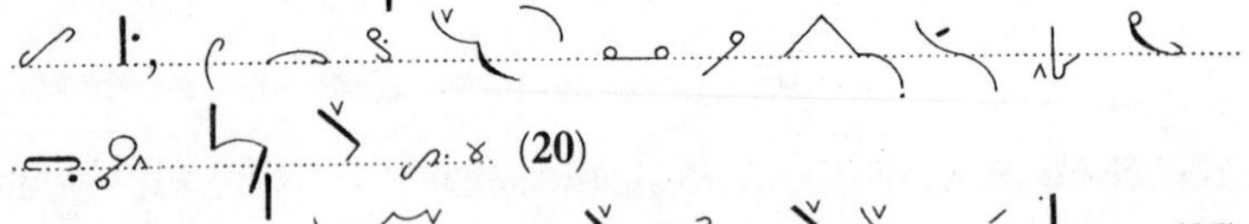

2 (20)

3 32. (15)

4 32, (15)

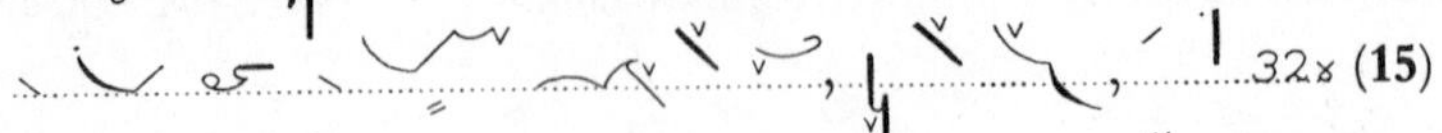

5 14, 7 1976 (27)

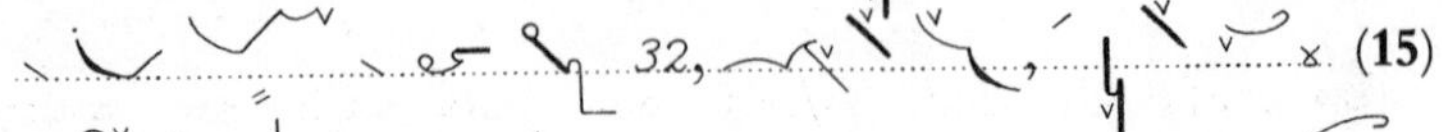

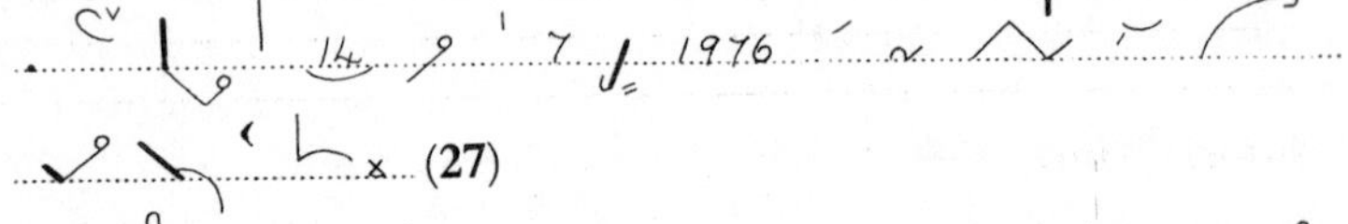

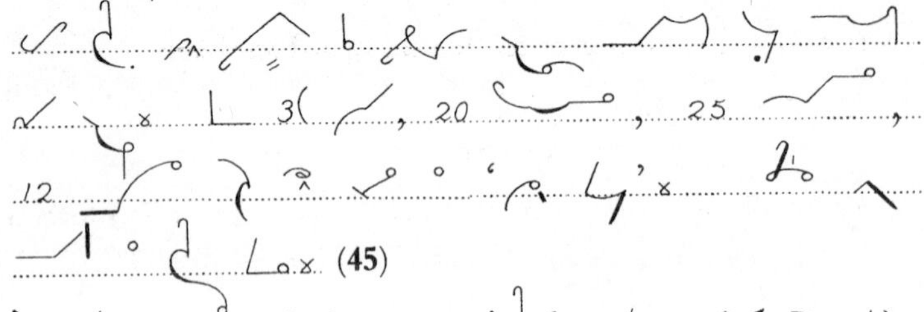

6 3(, 20 , 25 , 12 (45)

7 2½ (26)

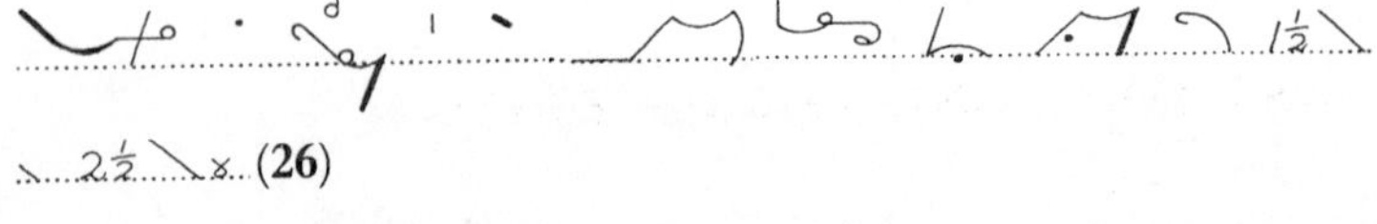

Key to Theory Drill

1 At one time 21 was regarded as the coming / of age but now this event is celebrated on the / 18th birthday. (**22**)
2 One day, three men spent five or six hours repairing / four out of the seven greenhouses damaged by the wind. / (**20**)

3 To convert centigrade to Fahrenheit multiply by nine, divide by / five, and add 32. (**15**)

4 To convert Fahrenheit to centigrade subtract 32, multiply by / five, and divide by nine. (**15**)

5 The flight departs at 14.00 hours on 7 June / 1976 and you should report not / later than two hours before that time. (**27**)

6 When travelling round Europe it is useful to have some / currency for each country you are to visit. Take / 3000 lire, 20 francs, 25 marks, 12 guilders or / other amounts to use as 'loose change'. Larger sums should / be carried as travellers' cheques. (**45**)

7 Banks charge a percentage on all currency transactions which may / range from 1½ per cent to / 2½ per cent. (**26**)

Short Forms and Derivatives

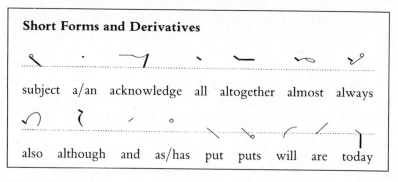

subject a/an acknowledge all altogether almost always

also although and as/has put puts will are today

Intersection

Stroke **T** ⌐ is intersected for the word *attention*:

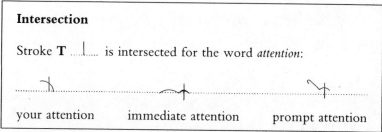

your attention   immediate attention   prompt attention

SHORT FORM AND PHRASE DRILL

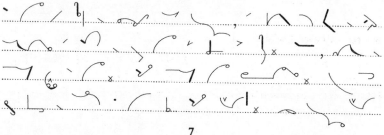

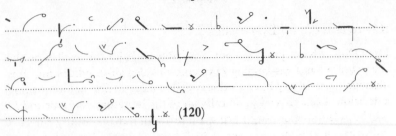

(120)

Key to Short Form and Phrase Drill

All letters are addressed to someone in the firm, and / it will be your job to open the envelopes and / also to put the letters on the desk of the / addressee. Altogether, you will have to acknowledge thousands of letters. / Always acknowledge letters as quickly as possible. After action has / been taken to answer a letter it is always filed. / Most firms file all letters dealing with one subject together. / It is always a good idea to get to know / the rules for filing before you take charge of the / correspondence. It is almost impossible to lose any document in / the office if you always take care to file according / to the rules. Prompt attention to filing always pays dividends. / **(120)**

CORRESPONDENCE

Letter to:

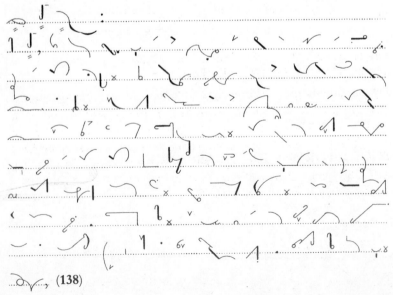

(138)

Chapter 1

Key to letter to Mr Don Irving:

Dear Don, Thank you for your brief note and all / the leaflets on the subject of oil and gas heating / systems and also air-conditioning. It is obviously useful to / have all the available information before making a decision. I / have read practically all of the literature you sent and / I will be able to make my choice with much / greater confidence now. I will put your wide experience to / good use and I will also take advantage of your / kind offer to call to see the system you have / already installed in your flat. Please acknowledge this letter. I / am not altogether certain that I am using the correct / address. I knew you and your wife were working in / a northern theatre but I had a slight problem reading / the handwritten address on your note. Yours sincerely, (**138**)

Memo:

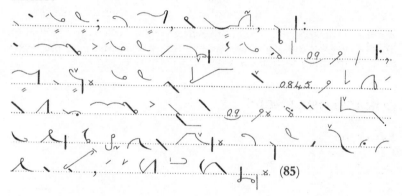

Key to memo to all Office Staff, from Manager, subject PUNCTUALITY, today's date:

All members of the office staff are reminded that the / office opens at 0900 hours each day, Monday / to Friday. Office staff should be at work by / 0845 hours at the latest and be ready / to meet members of the public by 0900 / hours. Complaints about bad timekeeping have been received and this / situation will have to be rectified. From today staff who / arrive late will receive two warnings, and on the third / occasion they will be dismissed. (**85**)

Letter to:

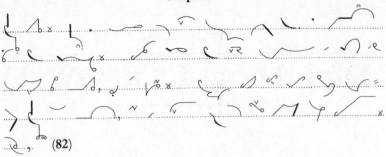

(82)

Key to letter to The Advertising Manager, Daily News:

Dear Sir, I wish to place an advertisement in your / newspaper and request that you let me have details of / the current advertising rates. During the next year my firm / will be having a regular sale every two months. We / sell almost every kind of furniture and also soft furnishings / such as curtains, sheets and towels. Frequently we shall want / to run special full-page advertisements in colour, and I / should like to have your price range for such work. / Yours faithfully, (82)

CHAPTER 2

Diphthongs I, OI, OW, U Triphones

The diphthongs **I** and **OI** and their triphones are written in the first place to the stroke:

bilingual	licence	smile	wise	survive	alive

reprisals	frighten	identify	identification	identical	oblige

either	crisis	entire	pride	deprive	whilst	fried	liable

priority	autobiography	diagonal	noisy	soil

boiler	hoist	loyal	royalist	buoyant	acquire

The diphthongs **OW** and **U** and their triphones are written in the third place to the stroke:

outlaw	council	doubtful	county	around	frown	plough	mountain

tower	drown	towel	allowance	lawsuit	cure	occupied	popular

11

Chapter 2

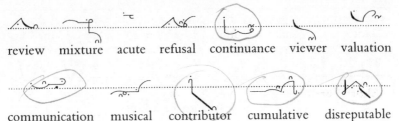

review mixture acute refusal continuance viewer valuation

communication musical contributor cumulative disreputable

THEORY DRILL

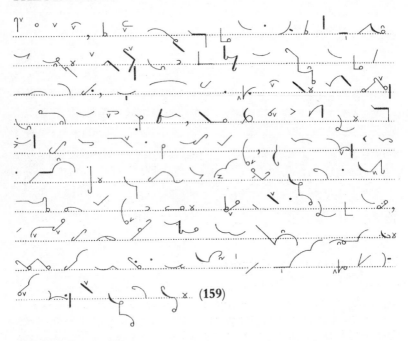

(159)

Key to Theory Drill

Try as I might, it is quite impossible to get / tickets for a show which has had good reviews in / the newspaper. I should be obliged if you would take / advantage of any opportunities for tickets which come your way, / no matter what the outlay might be. I will be / surprised if you secure any kind of seat just now, / because this is the height of the holiday season. I / get annoyed when I cannot occupy a seat in one / of our theatres, but then I am reminded that I / am not a regular attender. If it were not for / the loyal support of visitors from a variety of countries / some of our theatres would close. It is wise to / buy a season ticket for concerts, and likewise one must / reserve in advance

12

for any popular musical event. Perhaps we / will now place a new valuation on our cultural outlets / which are so highly esteemed by visitors from overseas. (**159**)

Short Forms

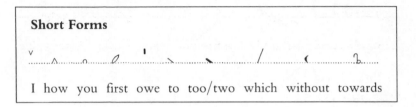

I   how   you   first   owe   to   too/two   which   without   towards

---

SHORT FORM AND PHRASE DRILL

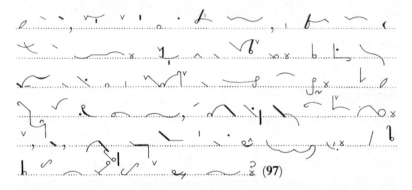

(**97**)

Key to Short Form and Phrase Drill

First of all, I know I owe you a large / sum of money, but just now I am without any / form of income. I do not know how to apologize / to you. It has taken far too long to pay / you but I hope you will try to understand my / situation. At the first opportunity I will save some money, / and you will be paid before more time elapses. I, / too, will be pleased to get back on to a / sound financial footing. Which address do you want me to / use when I send you the money? (**97**)

CORRESPONDENCE

Personal letter to Kate:

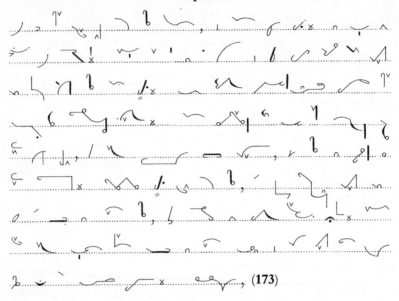

Key to personal letter:

Dear Kate, How delighted I was to receive your letter. / I first knew about your move to the Caribbean when / I met our mutual friend Jane, last February. She promised / she would try to find out your address for me, / but I am still waiting. You know how annoying she / can be! I know I owe you a letter but / just when I was about to write to you at / your old address I met Jane. Now that we have / renewed communications we must try to keep this correspondence alive. / I am surprised that you knew I had moved to / this quiet little town, which I have quickly grown to / like, but the address you used is quite correct. Perhaps / Jane found your address, and took the opportunity to write / to you first and give you my address, which would / explain how we have finally made contact. I now find / I have no more time to give you my news / but I will write more fully towards the end of / next week. Sincerely, **(173)**

Letter to:

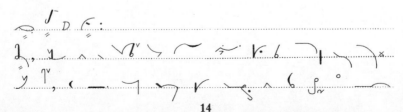

Chapter 2

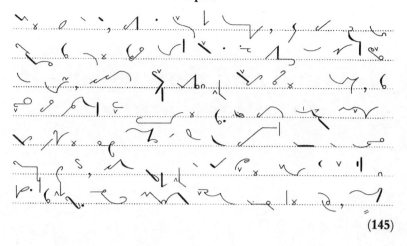

(145)

Key to letter to Mr John D. Lowe:

Dear Sir, I do not know how to apologize for / the long and annoying delay which has occurred to your / order. I shall try, without going into too much detail / to explain how this situation has come about. First of / all, we had a fire at the factory, without which / we would have had few problems this year. This was / followed by an acute reduction in oil supplies for fuel, / and we were obliged to reduce output by one half. / Fortunately, this crisis was resolved quite quickly. These events were / unavoidable and entirely beyond our control. Since then management and / staff have worked together to increase productivity throughout the plant, / and we have boosted the output of all our lines. / I felt that I owed you at least this brief / explanation and I hope you will be kind enough to / accept it. Yours faithfully, Manager (**145**)

Upward and downward R Strokes S and Z

R is written *upwards*:

1. At the *beginning* of an outline:

refer   rich   river   ruby   reservoir   requisition   respect   ransom

respective   respectively   recall   relatively   ridiculous   research   riot

2. In the *middle* of an outline:

barrier   card   modern   birth   partner   thoroughly   merger

certificate   pardon   parcel   awarded   carriage   charter   departure

3. When a vowel follows **R** at the *end* of an outline:

sorrow   boundary   Victoria   dairy   vary   marry   narrow

itinerary   et cetera   bureau   weary   enquiry   flowery

R is written *downwards*:

1. When a vowel precedes **R** at the *beginning* of an outline:

Ireland   aircraft   Eire   arson   era   orange   arrangements   architect

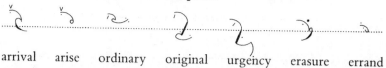

arrival   arise   ordinary   original   urgency   erasure   errand

2. When the sound of **R** *ends* a word:

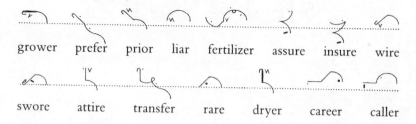

grower   prefer   prior   liar   fertilizer   assure   insure   wire

swore   attire   transfer   rare   dryer   career   caller

3. In the *middle* of an outline when the *root word* uses **downward R** at the end of an outline:

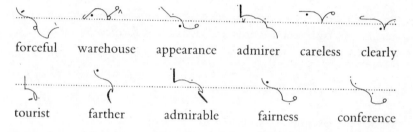

forceful   warehouse   appearance   admirer   careless   clearly

tourist   farther   admirable   fairness   conference

4. When **R**, initially circled or looped, is the only full–length stroke in an outline and is not followed by a vowel:

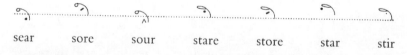

sear   sore   sour   stare   store   star   stir

5. When followed by **S** or **SES** circle or **ST** loop without a vowel following **R**:

burst   purses   endorse   worse   source   morse   curse   farce

6. *Always* before **M**:

boredom remarkable remember ceremony remedy aroma reminder

Chapter 3

STROKES S AND Z

Stroke S is used:

1. When **S** is the only consonant in a word:

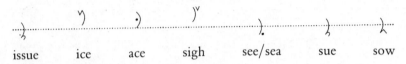

issue   ice   ace   sigh   see/sea   sue   sow

2. When a word begins with **S-vowel-S**:

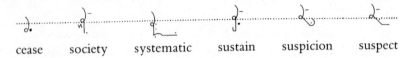

cease   society   systematic   sustain   suspicion   suspect

3. When stroke **S** is the first stroke in a root outline, the stroke is retained in compound words and derivatives formed by means of a prefix:

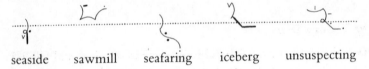

seaside   sawmill   seafaring   iceberg   unsuspecting

Stroke Z is used when **Z** is the only consonant in a word and when **Z** is the first sound in a word:

ooze easy zoo zeal Zambia Zurich zone zenith zodiac zebra zest

Stroke S or **Z** is used when a vowel precedes **S** or **Z** at the beginning of a word, and when a vowel follows **S** or **Z** at the end of a word:

ascertain astronaut astronomical isolate easily estimate oscillate

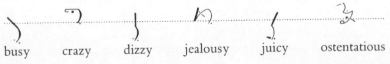

busy   crazy   dizzy   jealousy   juicy   ostentatious

THEORY DRILL

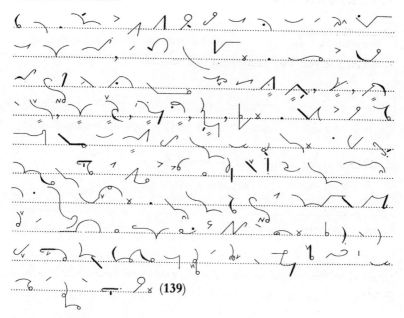

(139)

Key to Theory Drill

This year the aroma of the rich red roses was / in the air in and around the park in the / early morning, and also after dark. The names of the / various modern flowers conjure up rare pictures in the mind / —Red Ruby, Sherry, River of Fire, Early Arrival, Orange Star, / Astronaut, etc. The birth of the rose in this country / begins in March when firm new shoots appear. A thorough / pruning removes poor growths and the richness of the soil / is assisted by adding ordinary farm manure or an artificial / fertilizer. The pure form of these flowers and the remarkable / range of size and colour is clearly seen with the / return of summer. It is easy to see why growers / assemble themselves into societies and associations to exchange ideas and / information on new methods and systems of growing roses.   (139)

Short Forms and Derivatives

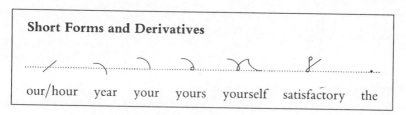

| our/hour | year | your | yours | yourself | satisfactory | the |

Intersection

Downward R ⌐ is intersected for the words *arrange/ arranged/arrangement*, and downward **R**, dot **ing** is intersected for *arranging*:

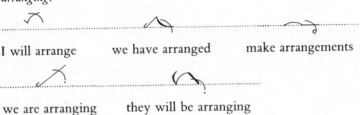

I will arrange   we have arranged   make arrangements

we are arranging   they will be arranging

Phrases

we are   if we are   we were   there are   they were   they were not

you are   are you   per year   last year

SHORT FORM AND PHRASE DRILL

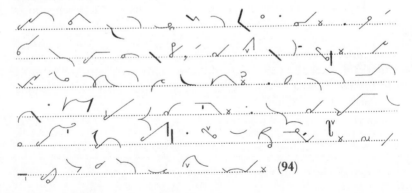

(94)

Key to Short Form and Phrase Drill

We were happy to have your news about your job / as a secretary. The hours and salary per week seem / to be satisfactory, and you are right to be so / pleased. Are you to run the office yourself or will / you have help? The first year of your career will / be a challenge but we are sure you will cope. / The firm you are to work for is well known / and they were awarded a prize in last year's export / drive. You have our good wishes for the start of / your new life tomorrow. (**94**)

CORRESPONDENCE

Letter to:

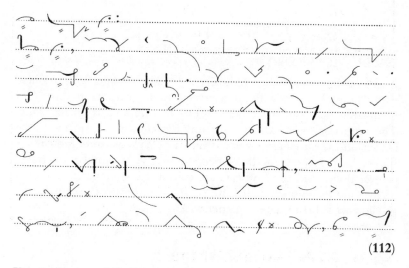

(**112**)

Key to letter to Miss Victoria Lee:

Dear Miss Lee, I am very sorry that your order / has taken so long but our factory in Kingston was / shut down during the early part of the year as / a result of an accident which injured several key workers. / We have had to arrange for some of our work / to be done at other factories and this has resulted / in further delays. As soon as our building opened again / your order received immediate attention, and I am certain the / goods will prove satisfactory. If there should be anything wrong / with any of the articles please let me know, and / replacements or repairs will be made without charge. Yours sincerely, / Sales Manager (**112**)

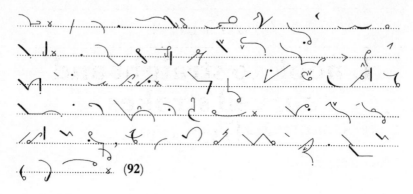

(92)

Key to 'Airport Inquiry':

Next month the new local authority will make arrangements to / hear complaints about low flying aircraft. Each year the number / of complaints increases and there are fears that nothing is / being done. The airport has been extended recently by acquiring / farmland to the south and the building of a new / runway. Package tours and charter flights have resulted in this / becoming a very popular air travel centre. Police and fire / officers are concerned about safety arrangements, and this inquiry will / also serve the purpose of reassuring the public about these / urgent matters. (92)

CHAPTER 4

L hook to straight and curved strokes
Suffix -ly

A *small* hook written at the beginning of a *straight stroke* on the same side as **circle S** is used for the representation of consonant plus **L**. The hook is used at the beginning or in the middle of an outline. **Circle S** is written inside the **L hook**:

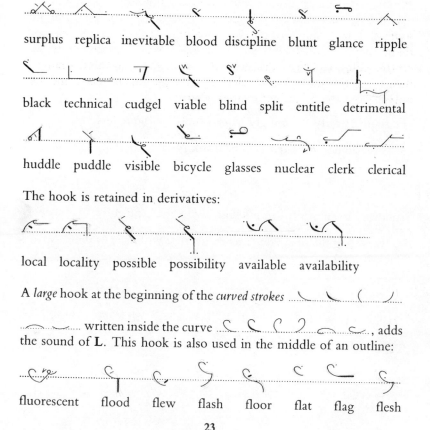

surplus replica inevitable blood discipline blunt glance ripple

black technical cudgel viable blind split entitle detrimental

huddle puddle visible bicycle glasses nuclear clerk clerical

The hook is retained in derivatives:

local locality possible possibility available availability

A *large* hook at the beginning of the *curved strokes*

written inside the curve , adds the sound of **L**. This hook is also used in the middle of an outline:

fluorescent flood flew flash floor flat flag flesh

23

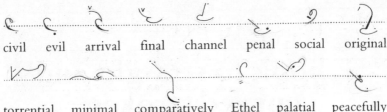

civil   evil   arrival   final   channel   penal   social   original

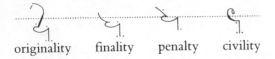

torrential   minimal   comparatively   Ethel   palatial   peacefully

The hook is retained in derivatives:

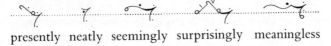

originality   finality   penalty   civility

SUFFIX –ly

The suffix **–ly** is indicated:

1. By **upward L** and the final vowel:

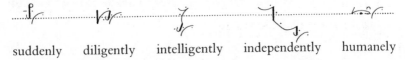

deeply   cheaply   hardly   calmly   warmly   freshly

2. By **downward L** and vowel, after **N** and **stroke ING**:

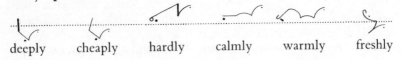

presently   neatly   seemingly   surprisingly   meaningless

3. By disjoined **upward L** after **hook N**:

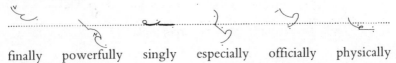

suddenly   diligently   intelligently   independently   humanely

4. By adding the final vowel when the root outline ends with a stroke hooked for **L:**

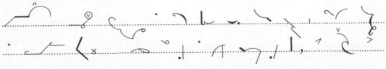

finally   powerfully   singly   especially   officially   physically

THEORY DRILL

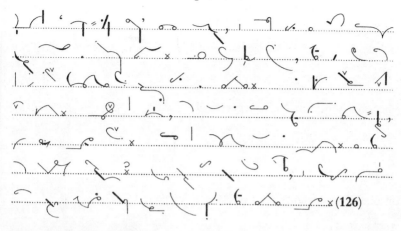

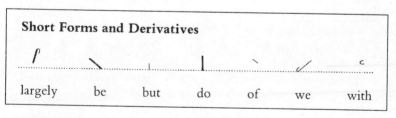

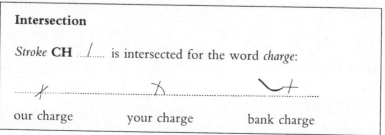 (126)

Key to Theory Drill

Regular exercise fulfils a very definite need for all people / but particularly for those who have a clerical job. Most / of us eat a little too much each day, and / the arrival of the so-called 'middle-aged spread' seems / inevitable, but extra weight is also clearly visible amongst the / comparatively young. Excess flesh does not flatter, and those who / suffer from it should apply themselves to clearing away the / surplus. A daily bicycle ride might help. Exercises at home, / or in a class for those lacking self-discipline, will / send the kilos flying. Glance at yourself in a mirror. / Is this your personal problem? Few people want to be / fashion models, but everyone looks more beautiful and feels better / physically after shedding those surplus kilos. **(126)**

Short Forms and Derivatives

largely	be	but	do	of	we	with

Intersection

Stroke **CH** is intersected for the word *charge*:

our charge	your charge	bank charge

25

SHORT FORM AND PHRASE DRILL

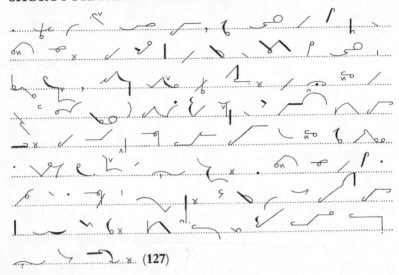

Key to Short Form and Phrase Drill

The new charges will apply next week, and these increases / are largely due to higher costs. We always do our / best to absorb such increases but it is not / possible every time, and we have had to revise our / charges radically. Our main clients are people with small businesses / so we feel that they are entitled to all the / regular help we can give. We carry out extra clerical / work for clients and this represents a personal saving of / time and money for them. The higher costs are largely / a result of an extra charge on import duty. With / the best will in the world we can do nothing / about this. It will be clear to you that we / are clerks collecting money for the government. (**127**)

CORRESPONDENCE

Letter to:

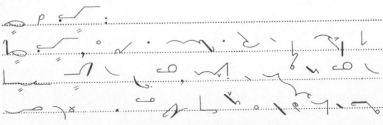

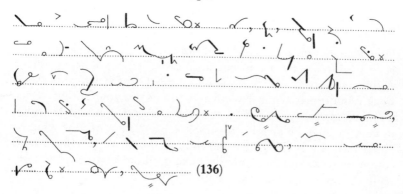

(136)

Key to letter to Mr P. Clark:

Dear Mr Clark, As you are a member of a / panel of teachers employed at the Technical College for evening / classes, I am writing to inform you about classes for / next year. The class usually taken by you is to / be split into two groups because of the increased demand / for places. You will, without doubt, be pleased to hear / that your class is so popular and I have no / doubt that you will be glad that such a change / is to take place. This was not my original intention / but a glance at the numbers already registered makes it / very plain that the proposed plan is essential. The Civil / Service Clerical Examinations, for which you prepare candidates, are to / be given new titles and syllabuses, and I am enclosing / details of these. Yours sincerely, Principal (**136**)

Letter to:

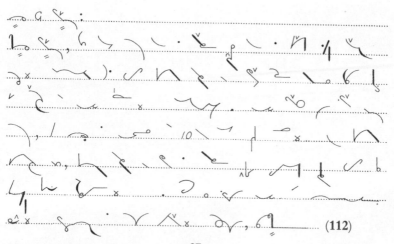

(112)

Key to letter to Miss G. Player:

Dear Miss Player, Thank you for the order for a / bicycle suitable for a child aged five years. I am / unable to say when it will be possible to supply / the article because this will depend on the arrival of / new stock. Unfortunately the new prices will apply to your / order, which means an increase of 10 per cent in / the total cost. If it will be helpful to you, / it may be possible to supply a bicycle out of / the window display when it is changed at the end / of this week. The machine is completely new and mechanically / sound. Please let me have an early reply. Yours sincerely, / Sales Director (**112**)

Disjoining T, D or Ed Half-length strokes Disjoining half-length T Md and Nd

Past tenses are represented by writing a disjoined **T** or **D** (whichever is sounded) close to the root outline:

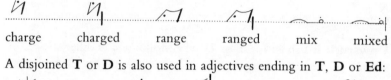

| charge | charged | range | ranged | mix | mixed |

A disjoined **T** or **D** is also used in adjectives ending in **T**, **D** or **Ed**:

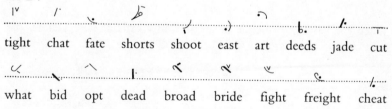

| unlicensed | unmarried | hurried | blessed | half-hearted |

HALF-LENGTH STROKES

In words of one syllable, without a final hook or joined diphthong in the outline, thin strokes are halved for **T** and thick strokes are halved for **D**:

| tight | chat | fate | shorts | shoot | east | art | deeds | jade | cut |

| what | bid | opt | dead | broad | bride | fight | freight | cheat |

In words of one syllable with a final hook or a finally joined diphthong in the outline, and in words of more than one syllable, thin or thick strokes are halved for **T** or **D**:

| find | paint | grant | doubt | secondly | parliament | impractical |

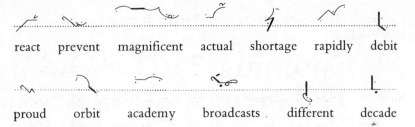

react   prevent   magnificent   actual   shortage   rapidly   debit

proud   orbit   academy   broadcasts   different   decade

Strokes are *not* halved when the halving would not clearly show:

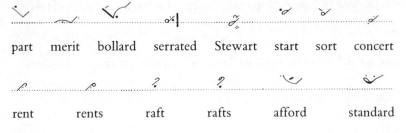

fact   flamboyant   probate   sympathetic   allocate   terminate

trumpet   platinum   victim   inmate   rampant

Upward R is halved for **T** or **D** when following another stroke, or when following an initial circle or loop, or when it has a final hook:

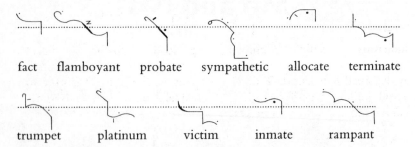

part   merit   bollard   serrated   Stewart   start   sort   concert

rent   rents   raft   rafts   afford   standard

When the halving principle is *not* used in words of one syllable, the root outline is retained in derivatives ending in **-LY**:

boldly   coldly   greatly   mildly   widely

A stroke is *not* halved at the end of an outline when a vowel follows **T** or **D**:

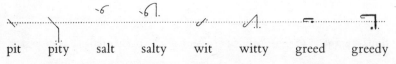

pit   pity   salt   salty   wit   witty   greed   greedy

Upward and downward **R** are not halved for **D** when a vowel comes between **R-D**:

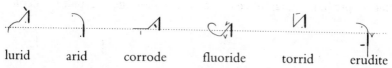

lurid arid corrode fluoride torrid erudite

Upward and downward **L** are not halved for **D** when a vowel comes between **L-D**:

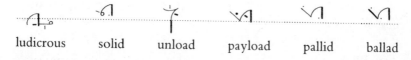

ludicrous solid unload payload pallid ballad

A disjoined half-length **T** or **D** following stroke **T** or **D** is used to avoid joining together strokes of unequal length, and in outlines containing a series of **Ts** or **Ds**:

substitute destitute attitude institute instituted astuteness irritating

Strokes **M** and **N** are halved and thickened to indicate a following **D**:

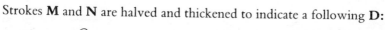

modern moderation madam indicate serenade thousand medicine

THEORY DRILL *Read*

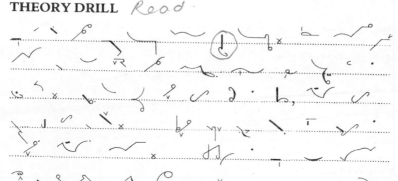

Chapter 5

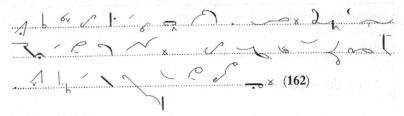

(162)

Key to Theory Drill

Good and bad results could be the effect of many / different factors. Stock markets react rapidly to any kind of / result and investing money is not for those with a / faint heart. Bids for shares rise when there is a / demand, and fall when people do not want to buy. / It is wise to try to avoid being caught between / a rising and falling market. It is certainly a good / thing to limit the amounts to be spent and prevent / heavy losses. Sometimes money is needed urgently for other reasons / and a cut in share prices has to be accepted / instead of a profit which might have been expected at / a later point in time. A share may reach its / height one day and hit ground level the next. There / is no doubt that money can be made and lost / very rapidly. When investing funds in shares you must adopt / the right attitude and be prepared for losses as well / as gains. **(162)**

Short Forms and Derivatives

able to	accord/according/according to	cannot

gentleman	gentlemen	immediate	immediately	particular

particulars	particularly	trade/toward	their	could

Intersection

Stroke B and **circle S** is intersected for the word *business*:

our business	their business	wholesale business	retail business

Phrases

Halving is used in phrases:

1. for the words *able to*:

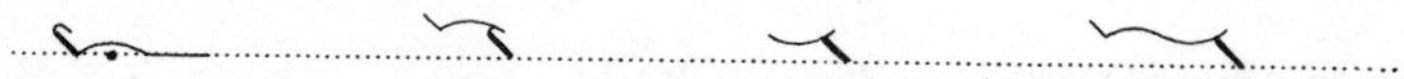

able to make   I am able to   unable to   I am unable to

2. for the word *time*:

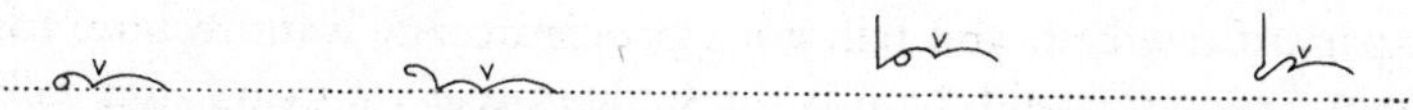

some time   from time to time   at the same time   at one time

3. with an **N hook** for the word *not*:

you are not   you will not be   and I do not know

but

    are not   will not

SHORT FORM AND PHRASE DRILL

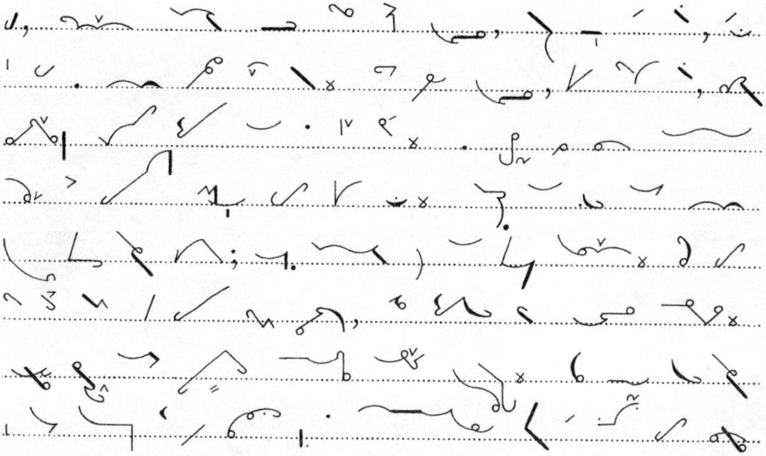

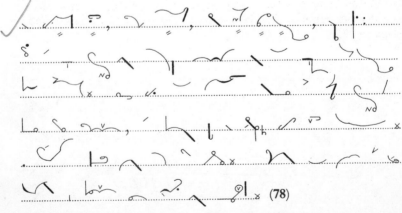

(198)

Key to Short Form and Phrase Drill

Gentlemen, From time to time I am able to give / particulars of the trade figures, both good and bad, and / comment on what the immediate results might be. According to / the recent figures, which are particularly bad, you will not / be surprised to learn that we are in a tight / spot. The situation is the same in many areas of / the world and I do not know when it will / end. I cannot see any event in the immediate future / which can possibly help; indeed I am unable to see / any change for some time. There is one particular point / about which we are proud however, and that is that / we have been able to increase exports. New business has / been found in all the European countries in spite of / the fierce competition. This could not have been possible but / for the fact that our salesmen did a magnificent job / and actually won some business from our chief competitor. Certainly / we would be foolish if we assumed that our business / could be better than theirs all over the world, but / in this area I would like to thank Mr Stewart, / in particular, for his efforts on our behalf. (198)

CORRESPONDENCE

Memo:

(78)

Chapter 5

Key to memo to Wendy Grant, from the Manager, subject
ANNUAL SALES CONFERENCE, today's date:

Plants and cut flowers should be ordered immediately to be / in good
time for the conference at the end of / the month. You cannot wait
any longer because of the / shortage of flowers which takes place from
time to time, / and it may be difficult to substitute one kind for /
another. The floral decorations will be your particular responsibility.
There / will be no limit on the funds available but at / the same time
some moderation should be exercised. (**78**)

Letter to:

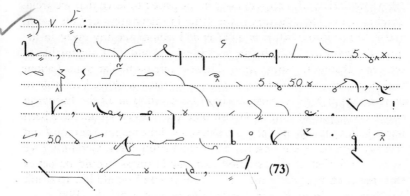

(73)

Key to letter to Mrs V. Short:

Dear Madam, Thank you for your letter received today with / the
enclosed cheque for £5. I must point out / that the actual cost of your
order amounts to £5.50. / However, to avoid any delay, I have sent /
you the goods today. I should appreciate your sending the / balance
owing—50 pence—within the next few days as / this will avoid a
considerable amount of book-keeping work. / Yours faithfully,
Manager (**73**)

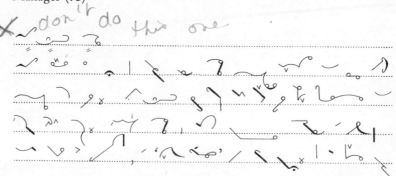

Chapter 5

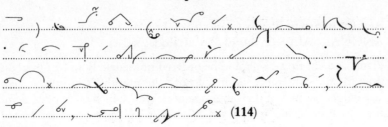

(114)

Key to 'Modern Communication Methods'

Modern science has made it possible to send messages many /
thousands of miles in seconds rather than minutes or hours. / Rapid
communication has been brought about by the use of / satellite
transmitters in orbit around the earth. Not only messages / but also
pictures can be sent and received in all / parts of the world, and 'live
broadcasts' are able to / be made. At all times people can see events
actually / happening thousands of miles away. This makes television
viewing a / lot more exciting and certainly makes the whole world
appear / a good deal smaller. Many business firms make use of / these
modern methods and, although the immediate costs are high, /
increased trade usually results. **(114)**

CHAPTER 6

H
Suffix -ship

H is represented by:

1. The sign ......✎...... written upwards at the beginning and in the middle of an outline:

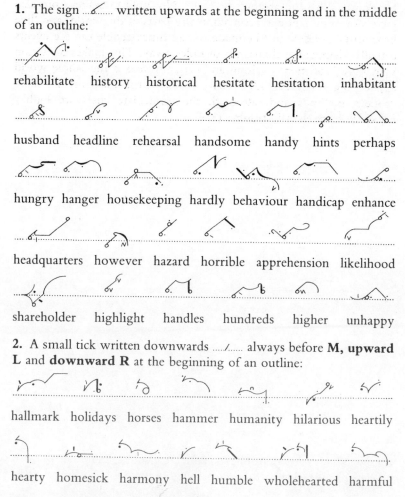

rehabilitate   history   historical   hesitate   hesitation   inhabitant

husband   headline   rehearsal   handsome   handy   hints   perhaps

hungry   hanger   housekeeping   hardly   behaviour   handicap   enhance

headquarters   however   hazard   horrible   apprehension   likelihood

shareholder   highlight   handles   hundreds   higher   unhappy

2. A small tick written downwards ......╱...... always before **M, upward L** and **downward R** at the beginning of an outline:

hallmark   holidays   horses   hammer   humanity   hilarious   heartily

hearty   homesick   harmony   hell   humble   wholehearted   harmful

37

When **H** follows circle **S** medially, the **H** is omitted:

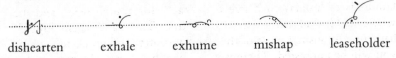

dishearten   exhale   exhume   mishap   leaseholder

At the beginning of an outline **stroke S** is used preceding the vowel before **H** as it is not possible to write a **circle S** before **H**:

Soho   Sahara

The suffix **-ship** is written with a joined or disjoined **SH**:

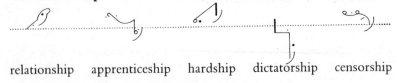

relationship   apprenticeship   hardship   dictatorship   censorship

THEORY DRILL

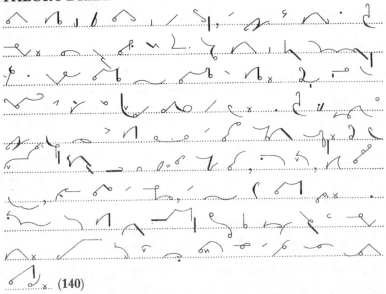

(140)

Key to Theory Drill

Happy holidays do not just happen but are planned, and / usually with the help of a travel expert. Some people / hesitate about asking for this help but it should be / remembered that such a person handles many hundreds of holidays. / There is no cause for apprehension and the whole of / his advisory services are free. The travel agent himself has / usually visited most of the holiday centres and hotels in / which you will be interested. There is every likelihood that / he will be able to give you first-hand knowledge / of the hotel, car hire, health hazards if any, local / habits and customs, and many other handy hints. The harmony / of your holiday will be guaranteed as far as it / is humanly possible with expert help. Working on your own / might mean higher costs and result in some unhappy hardships. / (**140**)

Short Forms and Derivatives

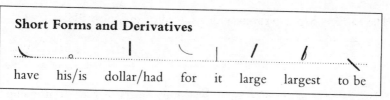

have	his/is	dollar/had	for	it	large	largest	to be

Intersection

Stroke **F** ⟍ is intersected for the word *form*:

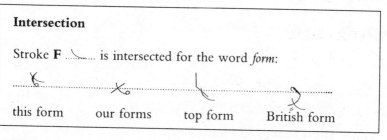

this form	our forms	top form	British form

Phrases

A heavy tick, written downwards, may be used for the word *he* in the *middle* or at the *end* of a phrase:

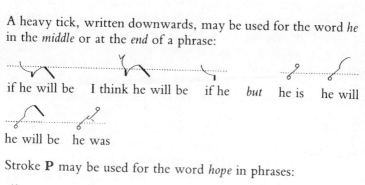

if he will be	I think he will be	if he	*but*	he is	he will

he will be	he was

Stroke **P** may be used for the word *hope* in phrases:

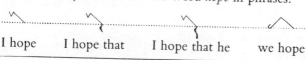

I hope	I hope that	I hope that he	we hope

Chapter 6

SHORT FORM AND PHRASE DRILL

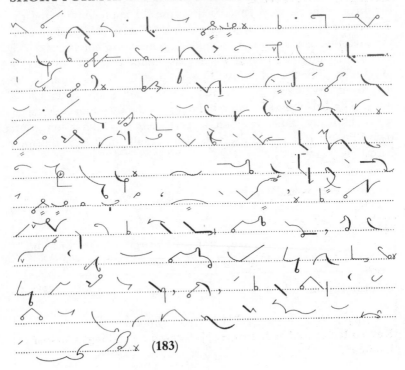

(**183**)

Key to Short Form and Phrase Drill

I hope Harry will be able to hear a debate / in the House of Commons. It is a great experience / to visit this historical place and it will be all / the more exciting if there is a debate going on / while he is there. It is one of the largest / buildings in London and he will not have to be / in a hurry if he wishes to take in every / detail of this fine assembly hall. Harry has always been / wholehearted in his support of this form of political debate / and I think he will be even more enthusiastic after / this visit. Many countries have adopted the British form of / government and the House of Commons is known as the / 'Mother of Parliaments'. It is hardly recognizable today from its / humble beginnings hundreds of years ago, and there is every / likelihood that within another hundred years further changes will have / taken place. Changes are not always for the better, however, / and it is to be hoped that what happens in / the future will help to bring about harmony in human / and international relationships. (**183**)

Chapter 6

CORRESPONDENCE

Letter to:

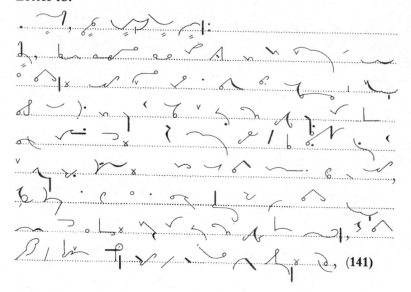

(141)

Key to letter to The Manager, Household Furnishings Company Limited:

Dear Sir, It is now six weeks since I last / wrote to you about my order and nothing has happened. / No-one likes to use a heavy hand in these / matters but I have no hesitation in saying to you / today that unless I hear from you within two days / I will take some form of legal action. Although my / order was not large it is hardly fair that I / should have had to wait so long. I am not / in the habit of making threats to anyone, and this / is not so much a threat as a simple declaration / of what will happen if no immediate action is taken. / I hope that I will hear from you within the / time mentioned, and that the happy relationship which at one / time existed between our two companies will be restored. Yours / faithfully, **(141)**

Memo to:

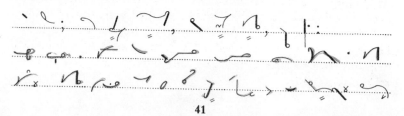

Chapter 6

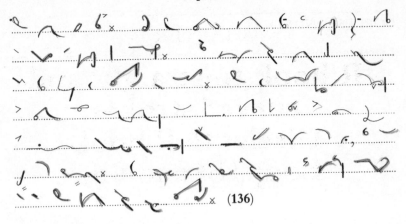

(136)

Key to memo to all staff; from General Manager, subject ANNUAL HOLIDAYS, today's date:

Instead of closing the whole company for two weeks next / summer there will be a holiday schedule. Holidays will commence / in the first half of June and continue to the / end of September. Senior staff will have first choice. There / is every hope of helping those with children so that / the holidays of parents and children do coincide. All that / is humanly possible will be done to bring about this / change without hardship to anyone. Staff without family commitments are / reminded of the heavy costs involved in taking holidays at / the height of the summer season and the economic benefits / to be gained by going away early or late, that / is in June or September. This new arrangement will present / problems but with the wholehearted co-operation of all staff it / will be possible to avoid hardships. **(136)**

CHAPTER 7

R hook to straight and curved strokes
Circles to R hook
Loops St and Ster

A *small* hook written at the *beginning* of a straight stroke on the left side and underneath straight horizontals is used for the representation of consonant plus **R**:

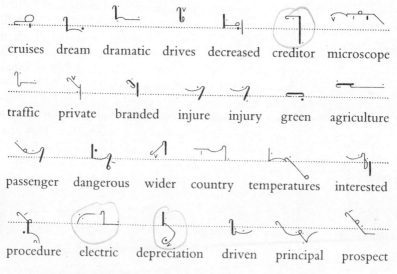

cruises dream dramatic drives decreased creditor microscope

traffic private branded injure injury green agriculture

passenger dangerous wider country temperatures interested

procedure electric depreciation driven principal prospect

At the beginning of an outline, **circle S** is added to straight strokes hooked for **R** by closing the hook. In such a combination, the **circle S** is read first. **Circle S** is shown inside the hook in the middle of an outline:

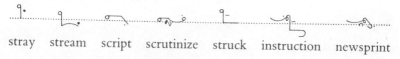

stray stream script scrutinize struck instruction newsprint

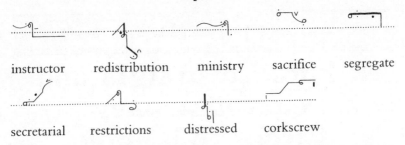

instructor	redistribution	ministry	sacrifice	segregate

secretarial	restrictions	distressed	corkscrew

When the sound of **SKR** or **SGR** follows **D, P** or **B** the hook and circle are written:

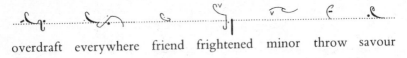

disgraced	subscription	prescription	discriminating	description

A *small* hook written at the *beginning* and *inside* a curve, adds the sound of **R** at the beginning or in the middle of an outline. **Circle S** is written inside the hook:

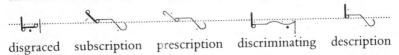

overdraft	everywhere	friend	frightened	minor	throw	savour

endeavour	brochures	consumer	rumour	throughout	innermost

When an unstressed vowel occurs between the consonant and the sound of **R** within a syllable, the **hook R** is used and the vowel is omitted:

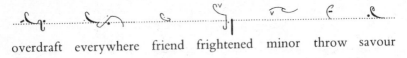

correction	directory	persuade	portray	forbid	decorate

opportune	murmur	perform	persist	vermilion	foresee

After straight upstrokes final **N-R** is written with **stroke N** and **downward R**:

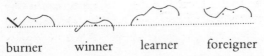

burner	winner	learner	foreigner

The **ST** loop may be written at the beginning, in the middle or at the end of an outline except when the outline begins or ends with a vowel. The **STER** loop is written in the middle or at the end of an outline:

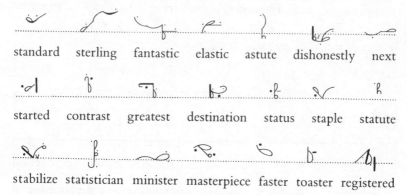

| standard | sterling | fantastic | elastic | astute | dishonestly | next |

| started | contrast | greatest | destination | status | staple | statute |

| stabilize | statistician | minister | masterpiece | faster | toaster | registered |

THEORY DRILL   *Read*

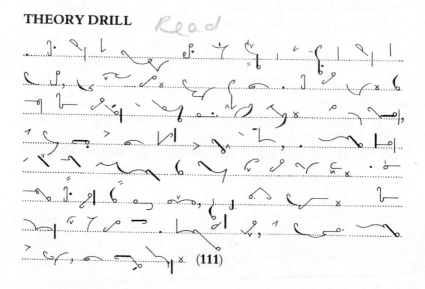

(111)

Key to Theory Drill

The train stopped at the principal stations only on Fridays / but on the other days it stopped at every station, / even the minor ones. Frequently throughout the summer the train / was full. This extra traffic was composed of passengers seeking / leisure and pleasure. As the year progressed, and the fresh / greens of the summer turned to the browns of autumn, / the numbers decreased and by October and November this branch / line was particularly quiet. A soccer express train used this / section sometimes, but this did not happen every week. Traffic / remained light until once again the temperatures started to rise, / and the ever-increasing numbers of the friendly, summer groups / appeared. (**111**)

Short Forms and Derivatives

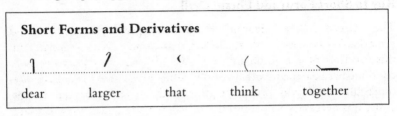

| dear | larger | that | think | together |

Intersections

Stroke **K** .... is intersected or written close to the preceding outline for the word *company*:

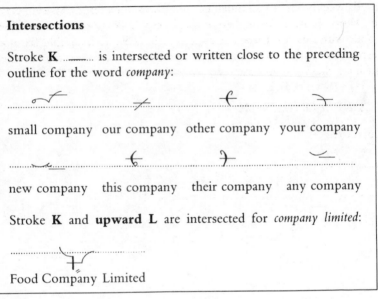

small company our company other company your company

new company this company their company any company

Stroke **K** and **upward L** are intersected for *company limited*:

Food Company Limited

SHORT FORM AND PHRASE DRILL Read

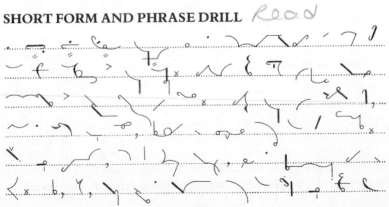

(127)

Key to Short Form and Phrase Drill

The Green Acre Frozen Food Company Limited is a remarkable / concern and much larger than any other company in this / section of the food industry. We feel that this growth / will continue because the members of the public prefer our / products. We think that food will always be dear, and / in an endeavour to cut costs, it is necessary to / scrutinize orders for large quantities. Buying goods weekly, or at / so much per month, is not a discriminating way to / shop. It is, I think, better to place a bulk / order for branded goods with this company every six months. / So far the public has not responded to this method / of purchasing, but I know that in this business there / is no other way to make economies. **(127)**

CORRESPONDENCE

Letter to:

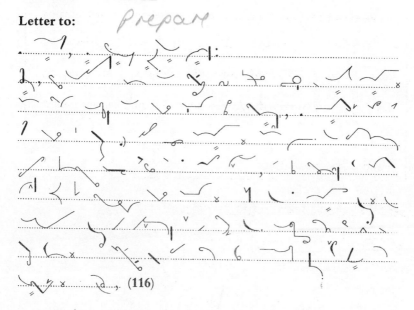

(116)

Key to letter to The Manager, The French Shipping Company Limited:

Dear Sir, Please forward to me any brochures you have / on your company's cruises to North America. I am particularly / interested in ports of call such as Bermuda, the Caribbean / islands and the larger ports on both the east and / west coasts of America. I am looking for warmer winter / temperatures together with all the comforts of a modern liner, / and it is presumed that I will be allowed ashore / at the principal ports of call. I do have an / American visa. If any further visas are required I should / appreciate having instructions from you as to how to obtain / them. I propose to be away from this country during / either January or February. Yours faithfully, (**116**)

Letter to:

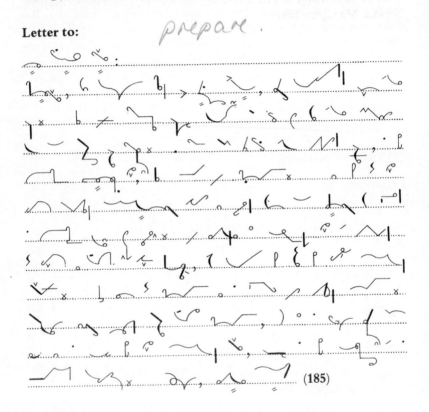

prepare.

(**185**)

Key to letter to Miss Frances Price:

Dear Miss Price, Thank you for your letter addressed to / the Chairman of the Company, which has been forwarded to / my office today. It is our company practice to deal / with virtually all complaints through this office and I hope / you will not have any objection to this procedure. The / product about which you complain and have returned to this / company, a set of electric Christmas tree lights, does carry / our trade mark. You state that the lights were purchased / in November and when you used them in December they / caused an electrical fuse throughout the house. Our service department / has inspected the lights and reported that the wiring is / faulty and quite dangerous, and they further state that this / set was not manufactured by our company. It would seem / that the trade mark is a copy of our own / registered mark. Obviously you have been misled by this false / trade mark, so as a friendly gesture I am sending / you a new set of lights manufactured by us, together / with a set of instructions and a guarantee for one / year. Yours sincerely, Service Manager (**185**)

CHAPTER 8

N hook
Circles and loops and
N hook
Suffix -ment
Downward L

A *small* hook written inside the *end* of a curved stroke adds the final sound of **N**:

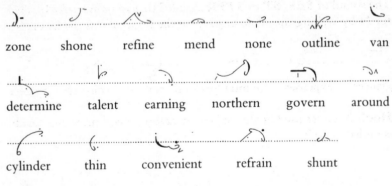

zone	shone	refine	mend	none	outline	van

determine	talent	earning	northern	govern	around

cylinder	thin	convenient	refrain	shunt

Circle S, reduced in size, is written *inside* **hook N** at the end of a *curved* stroke for the sound of **NZ**:

funds	assigns	telephones	shines	means	lens

Hook N is not used for the light sound of **NS** or **NSES** after curved strokes:

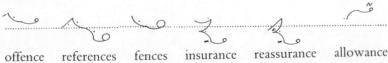

offence	references	fences	insurance	reassurance	allowance

A *small* hook at the end of a straight stroke, written on the opposite side to the **circle S**, adds **N**:

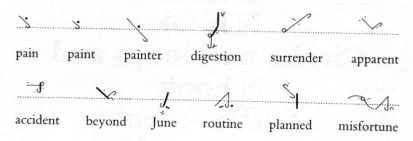

pain   paint   painter   digestion   surrender   apparent

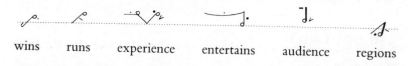

accident   beyond   June   routine   planned   misfortune

Circle S is added to **hook N** to straight strokes by closing the hook for the sound of **NS** or **NZ**:

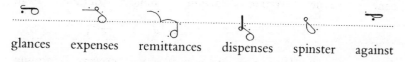

wins   runs   experience   entertains   audience   regions

The sound of **SES**, **ST** or **STER** is added to a straight stroke hooked for **N** by writing the circle or loop on the same side as the **hook N**:

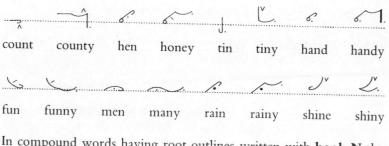

glances   expenses   remittances   dispenses   spinster   against

Hook N is *not* used at the end of an outline when there is a finally sounded vowel:

count   county   hen   honey   tin   tiny   hand   handy

fun   funny   men   many   rain   rainy   shine   shiny

In compound words having root outlines written with **hook N** the hook is retained:

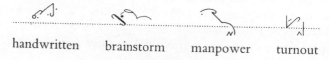

handwritten   brainstorm   manpower   turnout

The suffix *-ment* is written by joining  or, when not convenient,

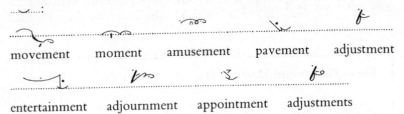

movement	moment	amusement	pavement	adjustment

entertainment	adjournment	appointment	adjustments

Downward L is always written after stroke **N, N** *halved*, **N** *doubled*, **N** initially hooked, and stroke **ING**:

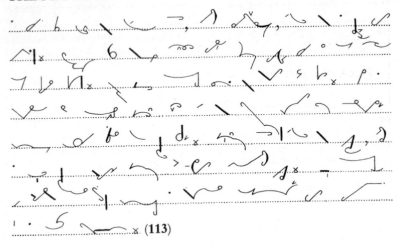

nail	neatly	endless	natural	mineral	amazingly

THEORY DRILL

× (113)

Key to Theory Drill

A story which you found to be funny can, rather / surprisingly, often be a disappointment when repeated. Frequently this is / because the amusement was not so much within the story / as in the manner in which it was told. People / who can entertain seem to be born with the talent. / Such a person has to understand the human mind and / be prepared to learn from experience to make the necessary / adjustments for different audiences. Humour can often be regional, and / there is a known difference between the humour of the / southern and northern regions. Good entertainment should always be planned / to maintain a balance in the material when working on / a national programme. (**113**)

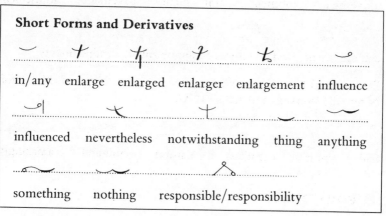

Short Forms and Derivatives

in/any   enlarge   enlarged   enlarger   enlargement   influence

influenced   nevertheless   notwithstanding   thing   anything

something   nothing   responsible/responsibility

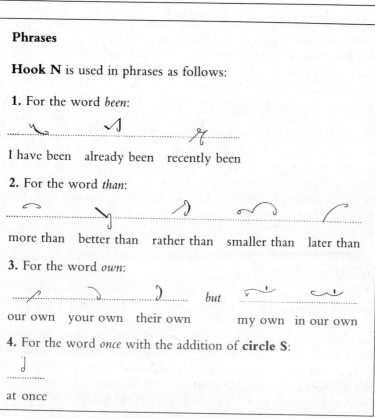

Phrases

Hook N is used in phrases as follows:

1. For the word *been*:

I have been   already been   recently been

2. For the word *than*:

more than   better than   rather than   smaller than   later than

3. For the word *own*:

our own   your own   their own   *but*   my own   in our own

4. For the word *once* with the addition of **circle S**:

at once

SHORT FORM AND PHRASE DRILL

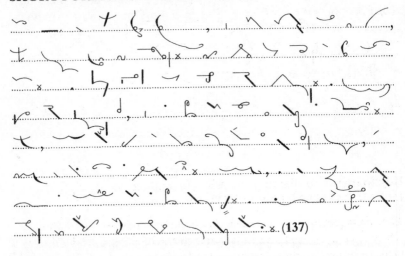

Key to Short Form and Phrase Drill

I am not going to enlarge on this point this / afternoon, but I hope I will be able to influence / you later, notwithstanding the firm views you have expressed. You / are not responsible for the actions of others any more / than I am. The damage caused in the accident can / be repaired. The financial details cannot be determined at once, / but a settlement about costs is better than an argument. / Nevertheless, anything by way of payment from your own pocket / has to be assessed fairly, and you should not have / to pay more than a reasonable amount. In any event, / the two insurance companies should be able to make an / announcement about a settlement before June. The economics of the / situation will be explained to you by one of their / own experts far better than by me. (**137**)

CORRESPONDENCE

Memo to:

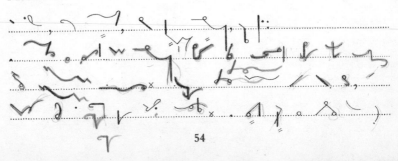

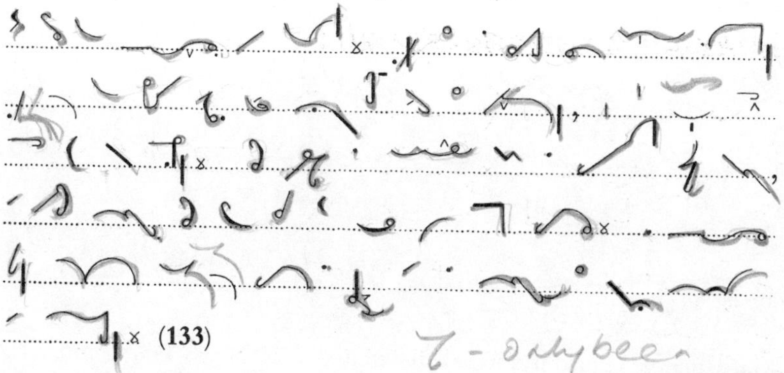

[shorthand] (133)

[handwritten: 7 - only been]

Key to memo to all staff, from Manager, subject *[handwritten: tape 74]* DEPARTMENTAL EXPENDITURE, today's date:

The management is concerned about the expenditure on stationery which / has increased suddenly notwithstanding the introduction of plans to bring / about economies. Evidently large sums of money are being spent, / and apparently there is a great deal of waste in / some departments. The Head of each Department is responsible for / seeing that the plans for economizing are followed. Each department / has a certain sum of money allocated each year for / stationery and these funds may be drawn upon as required, / but on no account can they be exceeded. There has / recently been an announcement about a world shortage of paper, / and rather than improving there is every chance that things / will get worse. The economies achieved earlier in the year / were a disappointment and an improvement has to be made / immediately and maintained. (**133**)

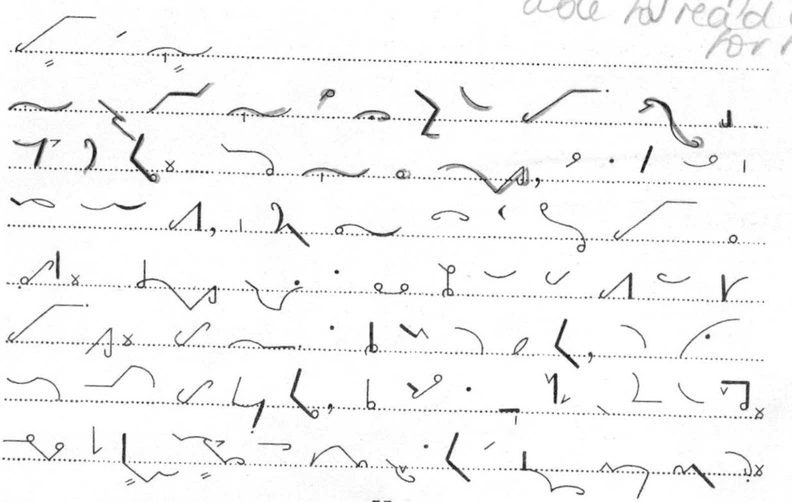

[handwritten: thoroughly be able to read it for tomorrow]

[shorthand]

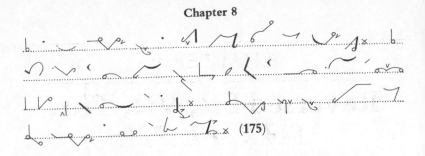

(175)

Key to 'Work and Money'

Many people regard money as the main object for working / and very often do not enjoy their jobs. Of course / money is important, and has a large influence on almost / anything we do, but there should be something more than / that as far as work is concerned. It is important / to feel a sense of satisfaction in what we do / in our daily working routine. When making a decision about / your first job, or later in your career when changing / jobs, it is always a good idea to ask for / guidance. Experts at the Department of Employment can help you / to find a job and determine how much you should / be earning. It is a common experience to find a / wide range of salaries in the various regions. It is / also apparent that some young people take the first job / that comes along and sometimes it turns out to be / something of a disappointment. It is important to try to / find work in which it is possible to experience a / sense of achievement and enjoyment. **(175)**

CHAPTER 9

Reversed FR, VR, Thr, THR, FL, VL

The curves **F, V, Th** and **TH** initially hooked for **R**, are always reversed after horizontal strokes and upstrokes:

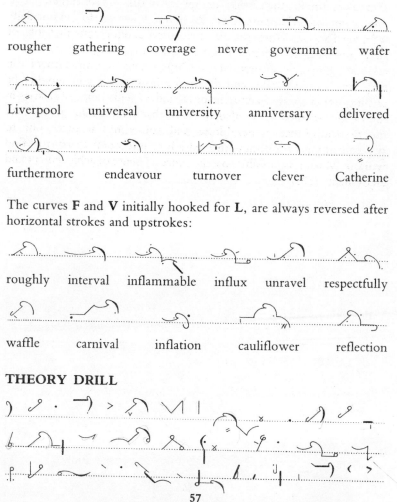

rougher   gathering   coverage   never   government   wafer

Liverpool   universal   university   anniversary   delivered

furthermore   endeavour   turnover   clever   Catherine

The curves **F** and **V** initially hooked for **L**, are always reversed after horizontal strokes and upstrokes:

roughly   interval   inflammable   influx   unravel   respectfully

waffle   carnival   inflation   cauliflower   reflection

THEORY DRILL

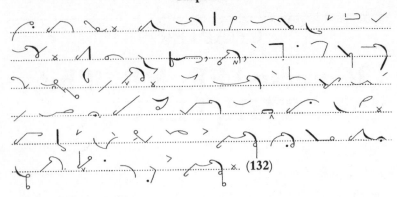

(132)

Key to Theory Drill

There was a gathering of the rival party at Liverpool. / The weather was good which is reflected in the marvellous / response they had. With such an influx into the city / it was something of a problem to discover just who / attended but I gather that all the leaders were present. / We have never had such numbers even on the occasion / of our anniversary. We do seem to have the distinction, / however, of getting a much better coverage from the newspapers / than our rivals. In the interval of time between now / and our next meeting we are anxious to recover any / ground we may have lost. We can depend on the / full support of most of the university leavers because we / have made visits roughly twice a year to each of / the universities. **(132)**

Short Forms and Derivatives

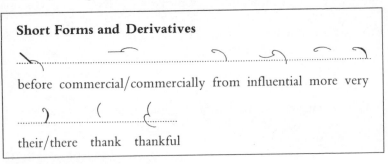

before   commercial/commercially   from   influential   more   very

their/there   thank   thankful

INTERSECTION

Stroke **K** hooked for **R** ⌐ is intersected for the word *corporation*:

large corporation   small corporation   this corporation

SHORT FORM AND PHRASE DRILL

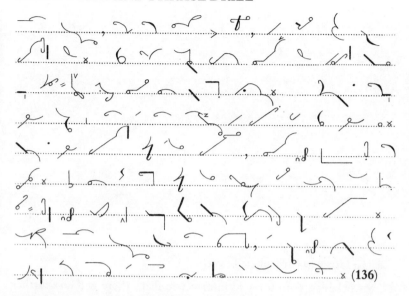

(136)

Key to Short Form and Phrase Drill

Commercial firms, from the very smallest to the largest corporations, / are always thankful to have well-trained staff. This is / particularly noticeable where secretarial staff are concerned because good shorthand- / typists and efficient secretaries seem to be getting rarer. There / may be a very good reason for this but more / and more employers are wondering what this reason is. Before / a recent world shortage of office workers, secretarial students took / their training very seriously. It would seem that the great / shortage of office personnel was influential in tempting half-trained / students to rush out to get jobs before they were / competent to do the work. In the last year commercial / firms have been more selective, and today's student will be / thankful that she completed her course and can meet the / demands of any company or corporation. (136)

CORRESPONDENCE

Letter to:

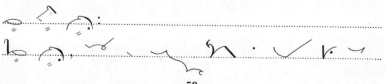

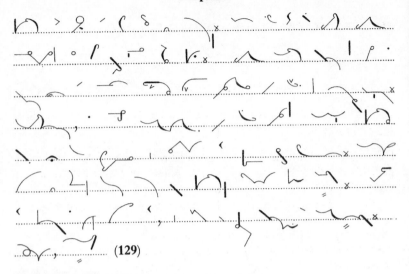

(129)

Key to letter to Mr Robert Lever:

Dear Mr Lever, I am sorry to inform you that / there will be a further delay in the delivery of / the roses and other plants you ordered. I am afraid / that the bad weather we have experienced has largely been / the cause of this delay. We have never before had / such a poor summer and commercial growers like ourselves are / finding it impossible to cope. Furthermore, an accident involving our / van resulted in no deliveries being made for three weeks / but happily that difficulty has been overcome. In your last / letter you asked for your order to be delivered promptly / at the end of October. I regret that it may / be a little later than that, but I hope to / dispatch before the end of November. Yours sincerely, Manager (**129**)

Letter to:

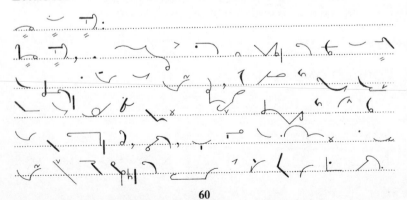

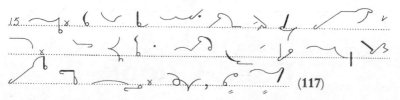

15. ... (117)

Key to Letter to Miss Ann Guthrie:

Dear Miss Guthrie, The manufacturers of the car you purchased / from this company in October have discovered a fault in / the fuel system, and they request that you bring the / vehicle back for the necessary adjustment to be made. Whilst / it is important that you allow this fault to be / corrected there is, however, no cause for alarm. A new / fuel pipe can be substituted very quickly and the whole / job will take roughly 15 minutes. This fault does not / in any way reflect upon the general workmanship on the / car. I can assure you that it is a marvellous / vehicle and it was manufactured by one of the world's / greatest motor corporations. Yours sincerely, Sales Manager (**117**)

CHAPTER 10

F and V hook

A *small* hook at the *end* of a straight stroke, on the **circle S** side, adds the sound of **F** or **V**. This hook can also be used in the middle of an outline. **Circle S** is written inside the hook:

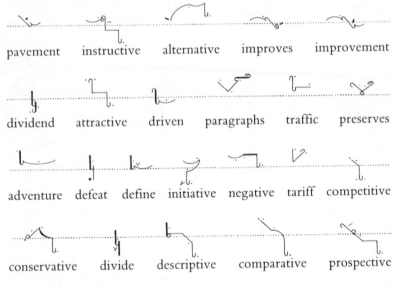

pavement   instructive   alternative   improves   improvement

dividend   attractive   driven   paragraphs   traffic   preserves

adventure defeat define initiative negative tariff competitive

conservative   divide   descriptive   comparative   prospective

When a root outline ends with the **F** or **V** hook, the curves **F** and **V** initially hooked for either **L** or **R** are written for the unstressed syllables *er*, *al*, *ly*:

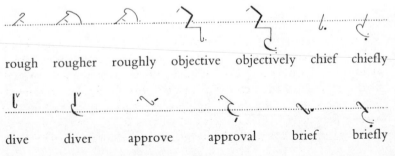

rough rougher roughly objective objectively chief chiefly

dive   diver   approve   approval   brief   briefly

When a root outline ends in **stroke V** following **circle S** or **SES**, add **upward L** for *-ly*:

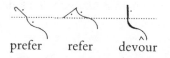

conclusively   excessively   decisively   permissively   evasively

When a stressed vowel or a diphthong occurs in the syllable **F-R** or **V-R** the hook is not used:

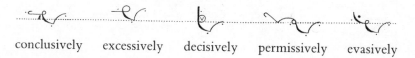

prefer   refer   devour

THEORY DRILL

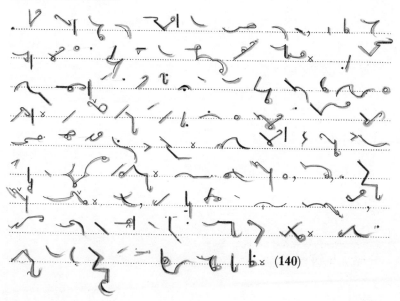

(140)

Key to Theory Drill

The tariff approved for this year can be used for / next year too, but it is only intended to serve / as a general guide for customers reserving in advance. Each / paragraph will have to be examined and a rough draft / made of any changes before this leaflet is reprinted. Our / prices are competitive and our chief aim is to preserve / a balance between increasing costs and what is fair to / the public. You will have observed that the profits of / the company and the dividends to shareholders are conservative. Making / some form of profit is, of course, the objective of / private enterprise. Nevertheless, we devote large sums of money to / improving standards, and we can never be accused of adopting / a negative approach to our business. We have a reputation / for thinking objectively and acting decisively in these difficult days. / (**140**)

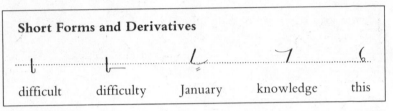

Short Forms and Derivatives

difficult	difficulty	January	knowledge	this

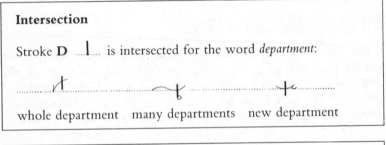

Intersection

Stroke **D** ⎯⎺⎯ is intersected for the word *department*:

whole department   many departments   new department

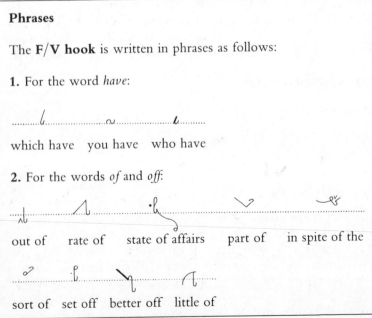

Phrases

The **F/V hook** is written in phrases as follows:

1. For the word *have*:

which have   you have   who have

2. For the words *of* and *off*:

out of   rate of   state of affairs   part of   in spite of the

sort of   set off   better off   little of

SHORT FORM AND PHRASE DRILL

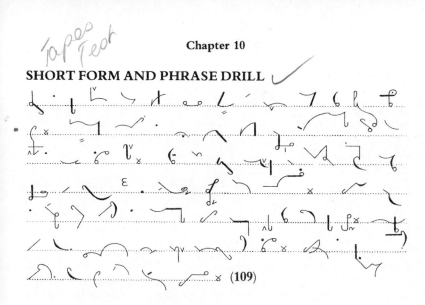

(109)

Key to Short Form and Phrase Drill

It has been a difficult time for the whole department / since January and to my knowledge this state of affairs / exists throughout the company. On Monday morning a meeting will / be held to discuss alternative plans for a new sales / drive. Those of you who have been invited to participate / actively in these discussions should bring with you the opinions / and suggestions of your colleagues. We need to have a / positive approach rather than a negative one to get out / of this very difficult situation. Many departments are having similar / meetings to try to improve their sales. We shall arrange / a departmental gathering roughly every three or four weeks. **(109)**

CORRESPONDENCE

Letter to:

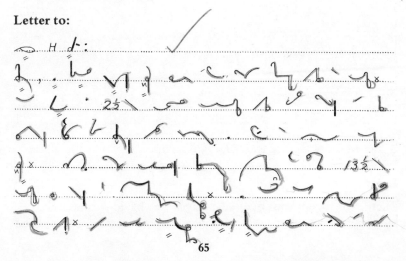

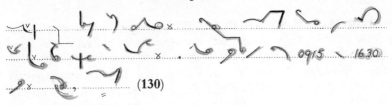

(**130**)

Key to letter to Mr H. Jones:

Dear Sir, The Advance Building Society is now offering particularly / attractive rates of interest. In January a $2\frac{1}{2}$ / per cent increase in interest rates was approved and / it is hoped that this will achieve the desired result / of improving the flow of money into the Society. You / will see from the enclosed descriptive literature that as much / as $13\frac{1}{2}$ per cent interest is paid / on long term deposits. The information in the leaflet deserves / careful reading. Our new Investment and Savings Department is now / open and you are invited to take advantage of their / services. Prospective mortgage applicants will also find the advice of / this new department of value. The office hours are from / 0915 to 1630 hours. Yours faithfully, Manager / (**130**)

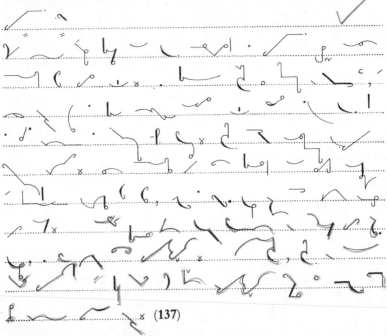

(**137**)

Key to 'Working Abroad'

There are many positive advantages in having experienced a working / situation in some country other than one's own. The adventure / of travel is attractive to begin with, and most people / think there is a definite improvement in one's own standards / after having had a chance to make a comparative study / overseas. Travelling can be instructive if we are prepared to / learn. Some countries are more advanced in certain industrial and / technical fields than others, and even a brief visit to / them can help to extend our own knowledge. In spite / of the difficulties which may have to be overcome to / arrange one of these visits, the effort will be more / than worthwhile. Alternatively, travelling to another part of the world / and devoting part of their time to worthwhile projects has / given great satisfaction to many young people. (137)

CHAPTER 11

Double-length strokes

Curved strokes are doubled in length for **TER, DER, THER** and **TURE**:

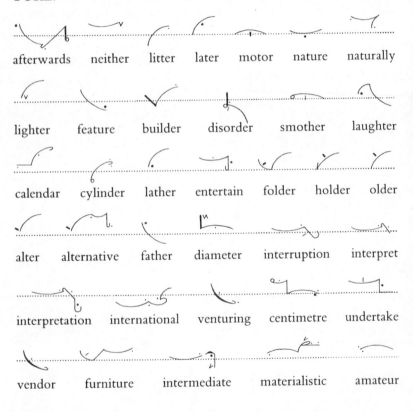

| afterwards | neither | litter | later | motor | nature | naturally |

| lighter | feature | builder | disorder | smother | laughter |

| calendar | cylinder | lather | entertain | folder | holder | older |

| alter | alternative | father | diameter | interruption | interpret |

| interpretation | international | venturing | centimetre | undertake |

| vendor | furniture | intermediate | materialistic | amateur |

Straight strokes are doubled in length for **TER, DER, THER** and **TURE** when they follow another stroke or have a final hook:

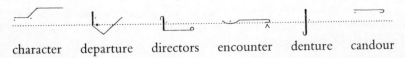

| character | departure | directors | encounter | denture | candour |

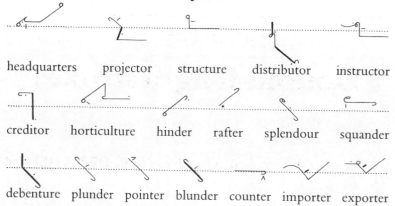

headquarters	projector	structure	distributor	instructor

creditor	horticulture	hinder	rafter	splendour	squander

debenture	plunder	pointer	blunder	counter	importer	exporter

THEORY DRILL

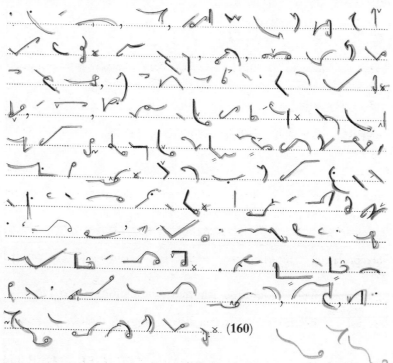

(160)

Key to Theory Drill

A father and mother, naturally, are concerned about the future / of their children and they try to render every assistance. / Young people today, however, sometimes feel that their parents cannot / possibly understand, and therefore cannot help in the choice of / a job or further training. It is wise, and kinder, / at least to listen to advice when it is offered. / Before venturing out into the work situation it is possible / to get advice from the Department of Employment where there / are experts who undertake such counselling. By the very nature / of their work they have to be up to date / with all matters relating to jobs. At school and college / there is usually a 'careers centre' and the operator is / a member of staff with an interest in further education / and careers guidance. The local Director of Education may set / up a headquarters for career counselling or, alternatively, hold an / annual conference for school leavers and their parents to attend. / (**160**)

Short Forms

wonderful	on	therefore	who

Intersection

Stroke N ﹏ is intersected for the words *enquire/enquiry: inquire/inquiry*

many enquiries	further enquiries	I will inquire

Phrases

A stroke may be doubled in length for the addition of *there*, *their*, or *other*:

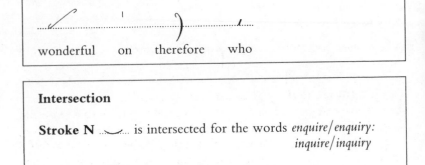

in their/there	in their own way	we know there is
some other way	if there is	we think there is

SHORT FORM AND PHRASE DRILL

(121)

Key to Short Form and Phrase Drill

There is a wonderful opportunity now to plan ahead. As / a result of the many enquiries we have made, and / on the interpretation of the figures available, we can press / on with the alterations. It will be possible, therefore, for / those who are responsible for the next stage to act / now. We know there is an opportunity here not to / be missed and I shall make further enquiries about alternative / methods of using the statistics we have. I will thank / each member of the wonderful team who were so successful / in obtaining this information. They always achieve excellent results in / their work, and if there is any special way in / which I can thank them I shall try to do / so. (**121**)

CORRESPONDENCE

Letter to:

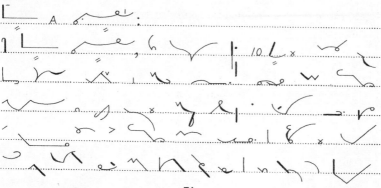

Chapter 11

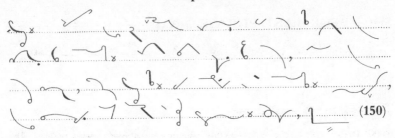

(150)

Key to letter to Dr A. Henderson:

Dear Dr Henderson, Thank you for your letter dated 10 / January. I am sorry to have taken so long to / reply but I have been making some enquiries about the / equipment and furniture you wish to order. I have just / received a folder giving details and pictures of some of / the equipment and I am enclosing it with this letter. / Further information should be available soon and I hope it / will be possible to send it to you before your / departure overseas. I wonder if you would be kind enough / to let me know what your address will be after / you leave this country. I will be happy to deal / with this order, and any future orders you may have, / from your overseas address. We export to all countries. Meanwhile, / if there is some other way in which I can / be of assistance please let me know. Yours sincerely, Director / (**150**)

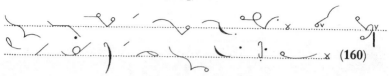

Key to 'Imports and Exports'

Both importers and exporters encounter many difficulties today. The importer / has to watch international money rates, which will affect the / whole structure of his large or small business. He has / to be able to interpret the signs he sees in / international trends and, like a doctor, check the temperature of / his patients regularly. The exporter must keep an eye on / the calendar to meet specified dates for overseas orders and / trust that there will be no interruption in the supply / and transportation of goods. If there is any delay his / work as a distributor is brought to a halt. He / receives a wide variety of enquiries, and every customer has / to be checked for credit worthiness so that he can / keep his business solvent. With so many problems to be / faced it takes a wonderful team spirit within any firm / to keep exports and imports moving successfully. Highly specialized staff / are necessary therefore and most firms have a training centre. / **(160)**

CHAPTER 12

Shun hook

The **SHUN hook** is written:

1. Inside curves:

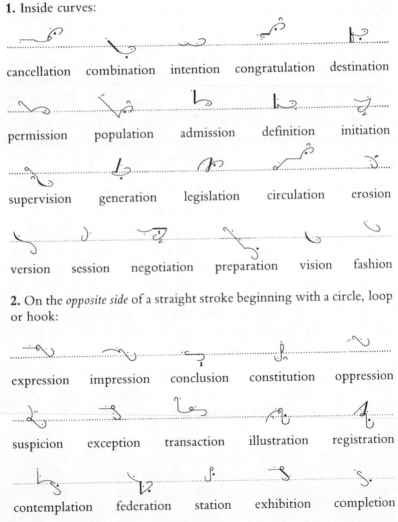

cancellation combination intention congratulation destination

permission population admission definition initiation

supervision generation legislation circulation erosion

version session negotiation preparation vision fashion

2. On the *opposite side* of a straight stroke beginning with a circle, loop or hook:

expression impression conclusion constitution oppression

suspicion exception transaction illustration registration

contemplation federation station exhibition completion

Chapter 12

To retain the **SHUN** hook in derivatives it is sometimes necessary to write the **hook** on the *same* side as the initial circle or loop:

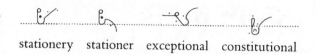

stationery   stationer   exceptional   constitutional

3. To a straight stroke on the *opposite side* to the *last* vowel:

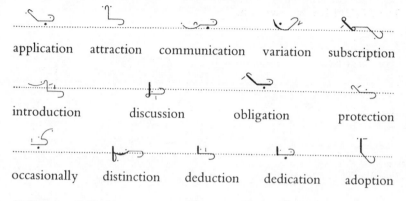

application   attraction   communication   variation   subscription

introduction   discussion   obligation   protection

occasionally   distinction   deduction   dedication   adoption

4. On the right-hand side of simple (without initial circle, loop or hook) **T, D** and **J**:

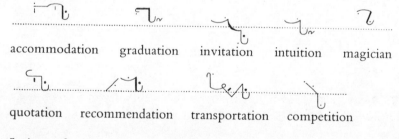

accommodation   graduation   invitation   intuition   magician

quotation   recommendation   transportation   competition

5. Away from a curve to balance the outline:

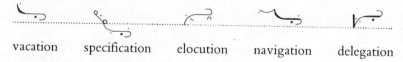

vacation   specification   elocution   navigation   delegation

The sound of **SHUN** following the **S, Z, NS** or **NZ** circle is written by continuing the circle through to the other side of the stroke. Third-position vowels are placed outside the hook, and when the hook is left unvocalized a second-position vowel is read between the circle and **SHUN**:

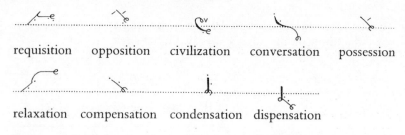

requisition   opposition   civilization   conversation   possession

relaxation   compensation   condensation   dispensation

Upward L following *S-SHUN* is joined or disjoined:

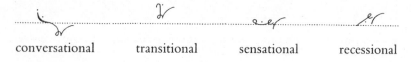

conversational   transitional   sensational   recessional

THEORY DRILL

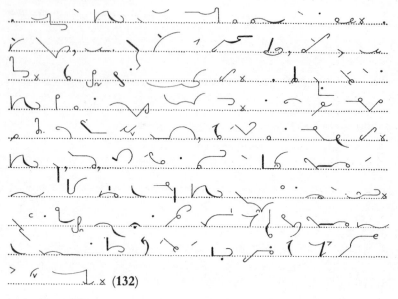

(132)

Key to Theory Drill

The introduction of television to any country is something of / a sensation. The whole population, including both the older and / the younger generations, surrender to the new attraction. This situation / has been an international one. The decision to take possession / of a television set is an important family action. A / more recent experience is the transition from black and white / to colour, and this operation is an expensive one. Television / today, of course, also offers a selection of educational programmes / and many additional homes have accepted television purely as a / means of communication. People with a strong constitution may have / made a resolution to look only at these special programmes / but many have to make an admission that their opposition / and dedication weakens and they enjoy the relaxation of the / light entertainment. **(132)**

Short Forms

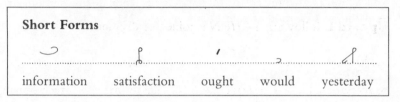

| information | satisfaction | ought | would | yesterday |

Intersection

Stroke **TH** is intersected for the word *month*:

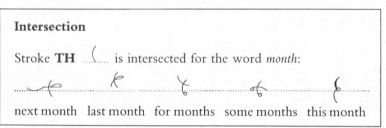

| next month | last month | for months | some months | this month |

SHORT FORM AND PHRASE DRILL

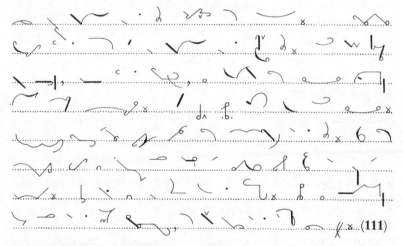

(111)

Key to Short Form and Phrase Drill

Most people belong to an association of one kind or / another. Perhaps everyone with a car ought to belong to / a drivers' association. Information about the advantages to be gained, / together with an application form, is available from centres located / along the major motorways. Large towns and cities also have / information centres. Financial protection and compensation usually result from membership / of an association. This is very important when you compare / the cost of goods and services yesterday with those of / today and tomorrow. It would pay you to ask for / a quotation. Satisfaction is guaranteed for the cost of an / annual subscription, or by payment of a modest sum each / month. (**111**)

CORRESPONDENCE

Letter to:

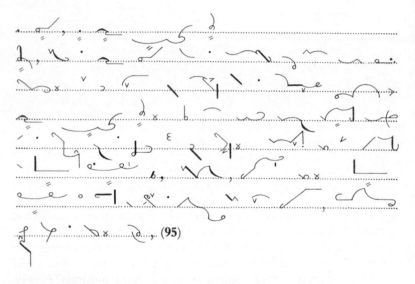

(**95**)

Key to letter to The Secretary, The Medical International Association

Dear Sir, I have been a medical secretary for a / number of years and I am now seeking promotion. I / would like to be employed by an organization similar to / the Medical International Association. It is my intention to move / to London next month and an opportunity to have a / discussion with you would be appreciated. I am writing to / you on the recommendation of Dr Sanderson who is, I / believe, well known to you. Dr Sanderson has agreed to / supply a reference about my work, qualifications and suitability for / such a post. Yours faithfully, (**95**)

Letter to:

(141)

Key to letter to The Manager, The Bookshop

Dear Sir, Would you please let me have full information / about the publication of any new books, particularly travel, history / and science fiction. You always have a fine selection, but / I have come to the conclusion that it takes too / much time to look at all the books put into / circulation each month, and if I had a list giving / details and recommendations it would be much easier for me. / Occasionally I have to purchase a large number of books / for distribution as prizes to school classes and I wonder / if you are in a position to offer discount if / the order is accompanied by a school requisition? Finally, do / you have in stock a copy of 'Twentieth Century British / Painters', which has lavish illustrations in full colour? It was / mentioned last month in the television programme 'Art Today'. Yours / faithfully, (141)

CHAPTER 13

KW, GW, WH

A large initial hook to strokes **K** and **G** adds **W**. **Circle S** is written inside the hook:

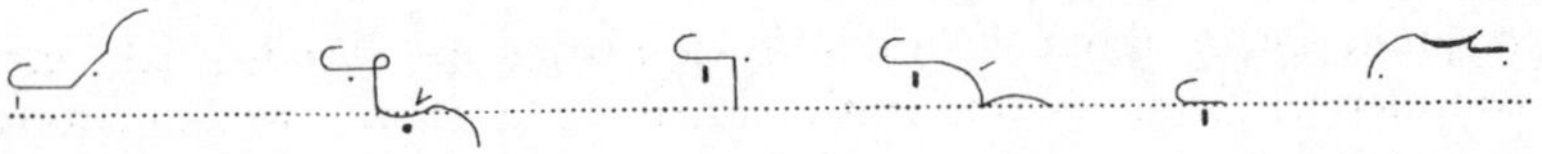

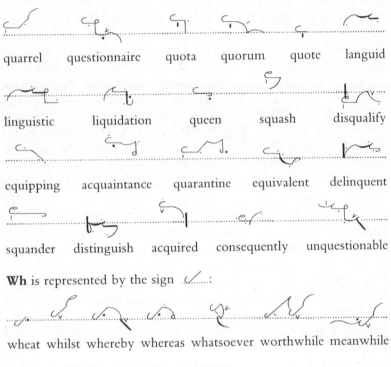

quarrel questionnaire quota quorum quote languid

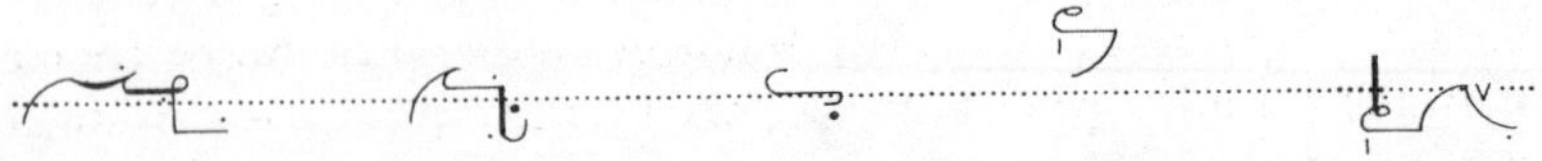

linguistic liquidation queen squash disqualify

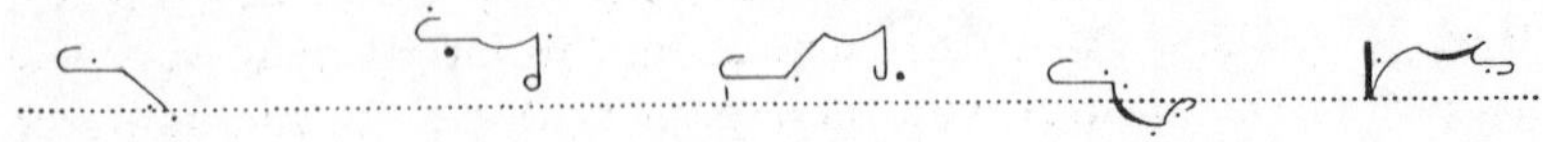

equipping acquaintance quarantine equivalent delinquent

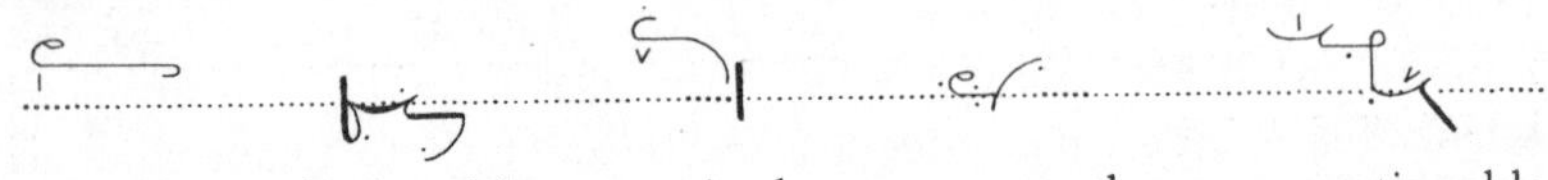

squander distinguish acquired consequently unquestionable

Wh is represented by the sign 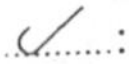:

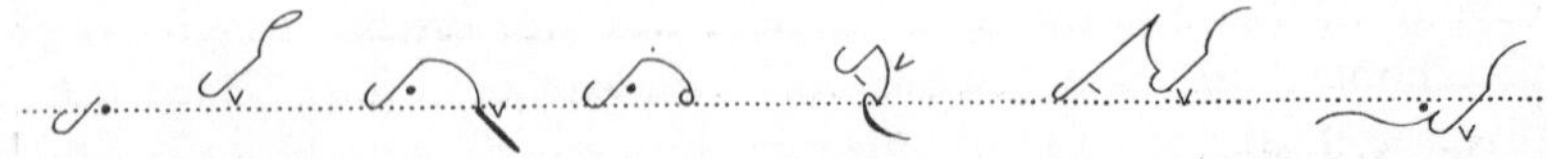

wheat whilst whereby whereas whatsoever worthwhile meanwhile

THEORY DRILL

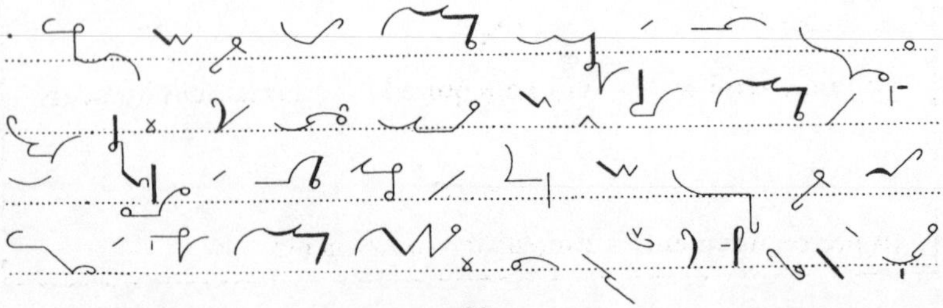

Chapter 13

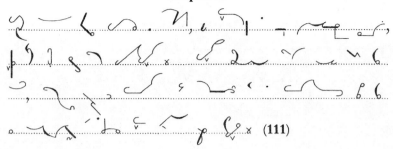 **(111)**

Key to Theory Drill

A questionnaire about the use of foreign languages in industrial / and commercial firms is frequently distributed. There are numerous enquiries / about how adequately languages are taught in schools and colleges / and questions are asked about the effective use of modern / equipment and costly language laboratories. Some people find their study / proves to be of no use whatsoever in their jobs / whereas the majority, who have acquired a good linguistic skill, / decide that their training has been very worthwhile. Whilst there / is nothing particularly new about this information, very few people / would quarrel with the argument that a qualification such as / this is invaluable and it seems quite wrong to suggest / otherwise.

(111)

Short Forms

manufacture   several   shall   should

Intersection

Upward R is intersected for the words *require/required/ requirement*:

you may require   will be required   special requirements

future requirements   immediate requirements

81

SHORT FORM AND PHRASE DRILL

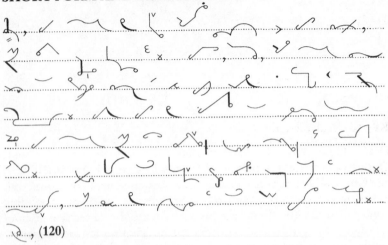

(120)

Key to Short Form and Phrase Drill

Dear Sir, We manufacture several types of wheels similar to / the one you may require, and I shall be happy / to discuss terms with you. We can, of course, always / manufacture something to meet any special requirements you may have / and should you wish to receive a quotation that can / be arranged very quickly. We have won several awards in / recent years for many of the goods we manufacture and / I shall be more than surprised if you are not / impressed with the quality and prices. If you require additional / information at any time please do not hesitate to get / in touch with me. Meanwhile, I shall send you several / leaflets with information about the wheels in question. Yours faithfully, / **(120)**

CORRESPONDENCE

A circular letter:

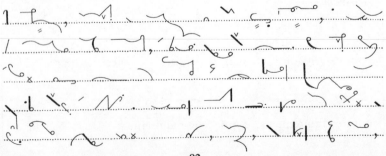

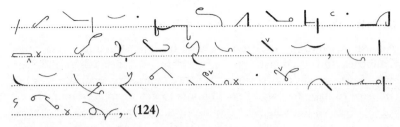

(**124**)

Key to circular letter:

Dear Customer, I am writing to inform you about Queen / Cosmetics, a new company which manufactures in this country, and / which is commencing business by making several exciting special offers. / You can make your acquaintance with the most advanced developments / in beauty aids by completing and returning the enclosed card / giving details of your particular requirements. Two free samples will / be sent to you. You will, I am sure, be / delighted with these products, each one packed in a distinctive / square red box decorated with a golden crown. Whilst there / is no obligation whatsoever for you to buy anything, if / you do have any future requirements I shall be happy / to supply you. A price list will be enclosed with / the samples. Yours sincerely, (**124**)

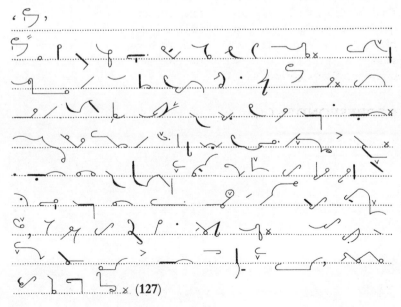

(**127**)

Chapter 13

Key to 'Squash'

Squash is said to be the fastest growing sport in / this and several other countries. Qualified instructors are in demand / everywhere and there is a shortage of squash courts. Where / courts are available it is not unusual to have to / wait several hours to get a game. Manufacturers of sports / equipment are finding it difficult to meet the ever-increasing / requirements of the public. The game seems to have developed / quite slowly from the time when it was used by / air crews to get some quick exercise and relaxation between / wartime flights, until recently when there has been such an / upsurge of interest. Anyone wishing to acquire the basic skill / of the game can do so quite quickly, and perhaps / that is one of its great attractions.

(127)

CHAPTER 14

Dot CON, COM Disjoining for CON, COM, CUM, COG Negative Words

The sounds **CON** and **COM** at the *beginning* of a word are indicated by a light dot written immediately before the beginning of the first stroke in the outline. The position of the outline is determined by the first vowel sound following **CON** or **COM**:

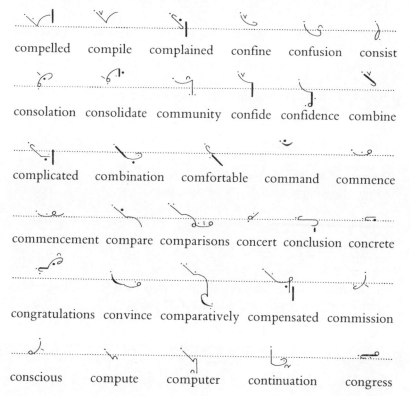

compelled	compile	complained	confine	confusion	consist
consolation	consolidate	community	confide	confidence	combine
complicated	combination	comfortable	command	commence	
commencement	compare	comparisons	concert	conclusion	concrete
congratulations	convince	comparatively	compensated	commission	
conscious	compute	computer	continuation	congress	

Chapter 14

The sounds **CON, COM, CUM** or **COG** in the *middle* of a word are indicated by disjoining and the dot is omitted. The second part of the outline is written close to the preceding part:

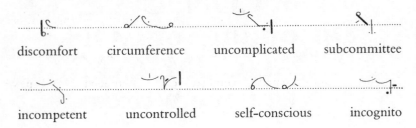

discomfort   circumference   uncomplicated   subcommittee

incompetent   uncontrolled   self-conscious   incognito

Phrases

CON or **COM** may be indicated in phrases by writing the part of the outline following the **CON** or **COM** close to the preceding outline and omitting the dot:

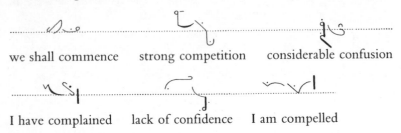

we shall commence   strong competition   considerable confusion

I have complained   lack of confidence   I am compelled

NEGATIVE WORDS

The strokes **M**, **N** and **upward L** are repeated to form the negatives in outlines beginning with **M**, **N** or **upward L**:

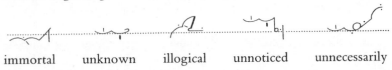

immortal   unknown   illogical   unnoticed   unnecessarily

The negative of an outline beginning with **upward R** is written with a **downward R** in front of the **upward R** stroke:

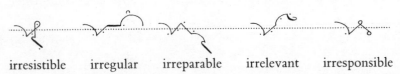

irresistible   irregular   irreparable   irrelevant   irresponsible

Chapter 14

Other negative words are written:

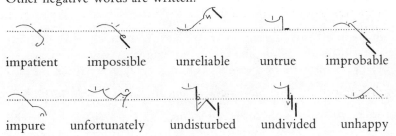

impatient   impossible   unreliable   untrue   improbable

impure   unfortunately   undisturbed   undivided   unhappy

When the prefix *IN* means *'not'*, **stroke n** is written:

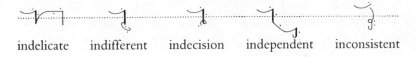

indelicate   indifferent   indecision   independent   inconsistent

THEORY DRILL

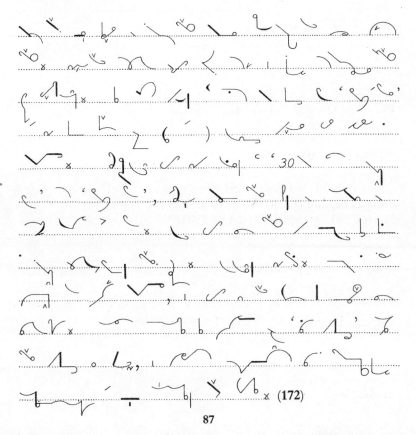

(172)

Chapter 14

Key to Theory Drill

Before buying goods it is wise to compare prices because / strong competition often means lower prices. You should not confine / yourself to one shopping area but continue your comparisons of / prices throughout the wider community. It is also recommended that / care be taken over 'special offers' and you should take / time to check these and see if you can recognize / what is and what is not a bargain. There is / considerable confusion when you are faced with '30 per cent / more powder free' or 'special offer', and there is no / basic price stated to enable you to measure the value / of the offer. Even when some prices are given it / would take a computer to solve the complicated pricing system. / If confused you should complain. Keep a constant look out / for real bargains, but when you find them do exercise / some self-control. In some countries it is illegal to / offer 'sale reductions' unless the price reduction is genuine, but / elsewhere irregular selling practices continue indiscriminately and go unnoticed by / the authorities. **(172)**

Short Form Derivatives

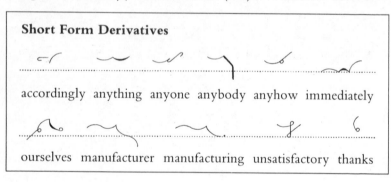

accordingly anything anyone anybody anyhow immediately

ourselves manufacturer manufacturing unsatisfactory thanks

SHORT FORM AND PHRASE DRILL

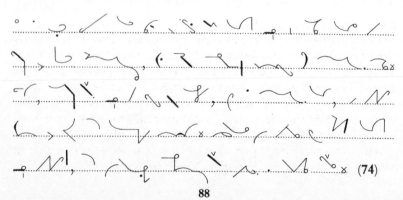

(74)

88

Chapter 14

Key to Short Form and Phrase Drill

As a nation we are often slow to complain about / faulty goods but unless faults are brought to the attention / of the manufacturers, they cannot be expected to improve their / manufacturing methods. Accordingly, anybody buying goods which prove to be / unsatisfactory, through a manufacturing fault, should return them to the / shop or factory immediately. Most companies will replace free of / charge faulty goods returned, or will compensate the customer by / refunding the purchase price. (**74**)

CORRESPONDENCE

Letter to:

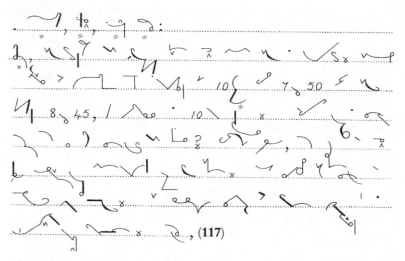

, (**117**)

Key to letter to The Manager, Accounts Department, Community Stores

Dear Sir, I have complained constantly about overcharging on my / account and now I have a further complaint. I understood / that the price of the electric kettle purchased on the / 10th January was £7.50 and yet I have / been charged £8.45, which represents a 10 / per cent difference. I wonder if this is a simple / error or is there some confusion about tax? Whatever the reason, your system of accounts does not inspire confidence and / I am compelled to check every item. In the circumstances / I think some form of explanation should be given. I / sincerely hope that all the blame will not be placed / on an unreliable computer programmer. Yours faithfully, (**117**)

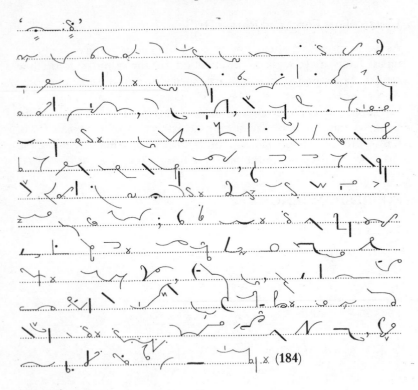

(184)

Key to 'Making Complaints'

You should not feel self-conscious or uncomfortable if you / have to make a complaint when there is good reason / for doing so. If you have ordered a hot meal / at an hotel and the food is served lukewarm, or / even cold, by indifferent staff the only commonsense thing to / do is to complain. If you purchase an item at / a shop which proves to be unsatisfactory it is only / reasonable to expect to be compensated in some way, but / this action can only be considered by the shop concerned / after you have made your complaint. There is no point / in complaining about the cause of the annoyance to your / friends and family; this achieves nothing. Complaints should be directed / to someone who can take positive action. In most communities / genuine cases of grievance receive prompt attention. Unfortunately there are / some, though comparatively few, people who do make false claims / supported by unreliable if not untrue statements. Comments should not / of course be confined to complaints. Complimentary remarks and congratulations / should be readily given, otherwise many deeds deserving praise and / thanks will go unnoticed. **(184)**